Penguin Health
Defeating Depression

Tony Lake qualified as a teacher in 1963, then studied psychology part-time at London University while teaching in children's homes and the children's department of a psychiatric hospital. He holds the degrees of B.A. and Ph.D. and is accredited as a counsellor by the British Association for Counselling. He is senior counsellor with the Centre for Professional Employment Counselling and is based at Sundridge Park Management Centre, where he trains managers from industry, commerce and the public services in the use of counselling skills. He is also in private practice as a psychotherapist, specializing in relationship problems. He broadcasts frequently and writes occasionally for a wide range of magazines and newspapers. His publications include *Affairs – the Anatomy of Extra-Marital Relationships* (co-author), *Test Your Sexuality*, *Relationships*, *Loneliness*, *How to Cope with Your Nerves* and *Living with Grief*.

TONY LAKE

DEFEATING DEPRESSION

PENGUIN BOOKS

To Katherine

Penguin Books Ltd, Harmondsworth, Middlesex, England
Viking Penguin Inc., 40 West 23rd Street, New York, New York 10010, U.S.A.
Penguin Books Australia Ltd, Ringwood, Victoria, Australia
Penguin Books Canada Ltd, 2801 John Street, Markham, Ontario, Canada L3R 1B4
Penguin Books (N.Z.) Ltd, 182–190 Wairau Road, Auckland 10, New Zealand

First published 1987

Filmset in 10/12 Monophoto Sabon

Made and printed in Great Britain by
Richard Clay Ltd, Bungay, Suffolk

CONTENTS

FOREWORD

This book has been written for three groups of people. The first consists of those who suffer directly from depression, and are puzzled and perplexed by it and want to know what to do to feel better. The second, are people who are concerned about somebody else who is depressed and would like to know more about how to help. And the third are those who want to be better informed generally about the subject.

Although the book is about depression and sets out to explain why people become depressed, its main purpose is not to describe the problem, but to explain in practical terms what to do to solve it. I do not believe in persuading people to 'cope' with depression, or to 'live with it' in the sense of modifying its effects so the misery is reduced to an 'acceptable' level. In my view, depression is something we have to defeat completely. No other objective is acceptable.

I hope the book will be useful to anybody who feels depressed, for whatever reason. When you have read it yourself I hope you will also persuade those who are concerned about you to read it too, so they can learn more about how to help you. At the very least, maybe they will understand more about how you feel and what makes you feel this way. But what I really hope for is that they will work with you to bring to an end the wasting years and begin a new future where depression is a thing of the past.

TONY LAKE
February 1987

Chapter One

WHAT IS DEPRESSION?

JUST A BAD PATCH?

There are times when we all feel deeply saddened by things that have happened recently, or go through phases when we are extremely miserable about life in general. If we tell some people about this they are quite likely to reply that this is part of the price of being human, and that no doubt we shall get over it. Are they right? Is this what is meant by 'suffering from depression'? Is it something we just have to accept, however difficult – a bad patch we need to get over as quickly as possible and put behind us without making too much of a fuss? Or is it something worse, a serious, genuine, full-blown 'medical' illness?

Behind questions like these there lies a widespread, but mistaken belief about depression. It is that the vast majority of people who feel 'down' are suffering from the emotional equivalent of the common cold – a condition which is inconvenient, incurable, but fairly trivial and goes away of its own accord. Really bad depression, it is said, is relatively rare – the mental illness equivalent, say, of pneumonia or tuberculosis.

Those who take this view are wrong. In almost every group of people you can meet there are some who are desperately unhappy, who can hardly cope with their misery, who have no confidence whatsoever that things will improve for them, but who manage to hide this most of the time. Such unhappiness is serious. It cannot be written off as 'just a bad patch'.

You may be one of these people yourself. If so, maybe you know why you are depressed. For example, your distress might be part of the aftermath of some recent personal tragedy, such as bereavement, separation, divorce, major surgery, or loss of a job. You will have an obvious explanation for your unhappiness which other people can sympathize with, although not for too long – they probably want you to pull yourself together and get over it soon. On the other hand, you may not know why you are so miserable. A very large proportion of those of us who feel depressed cannot understand or explain why, and our problem does not cease to exist just because there is no apparent reason for it, or because the reason seems trivial compared with the depth of the misery. Moreover, the lack of an explanation is likely to make us want to hide the problem, not just from other people, but from ourselves too. We are even more prone to do this when we are told by apparently well-meaning people that we are just going through a bad patch and need cheering up, or that we only have 'mild' depression.

The fact is, every form of depression traps its victims in a serious, recurrent, seemingly endless cycle of emotional distress. The length of time in which you feel trapped varies, of course, but even a brief experience of it can be devastating, and you cannot possibly predict how long it will last. The effect is that your life consists entirely of periods of desperate misery followed by times when you are barely able to cope, followed by more of the desperate misery. These are not the usual 'ups and downs' of life, but something much harder to deal with.

COPING AND CRISIS

The best times you ever experience are the 'ups', but these resemble most people's 'downs', because when you have them it is true that you can just about cope, but you are also aware of a sad difference between yourself and those around you which isolates you from them and often makes them think you are rejecting them. You feel tired and apathetic, dull and uninterested – that it is hard to gain any pleasure from anything, and that the occasional bit of fun is bound to be short-lived and not to be trusted as a sign of brighter days to come. So even at the best of times it is as though you dare not risk feeling good at all, because it will only lull you into a false sense of security and make the inevitable misery that is just round the corner seem even worse by contrast. Maybe you try to put on a brave face so that others will not see how bad you feel, or maybe you stop caring what other people think about you, but either way, depression dominates everything you do.

The 'down', or 'crisis', when it arrives, tends to affect every aspect of your being. It can attack you physically, so you feel ill and sick, weak and worn out, unable to sleep properly, but for no obvious physical reason. You are forced to use almost all your strength to carry out even the simplest task. It can destroy your self-confidence, making you stupid and unskilled, ignorant and clumsy, so that you are aware of being a danger to yourself and to others. You feel that all you have ever achieved up to now in your whole life is utterly trivial, that your capacity for doing anything worthwhile in the future, or knowing anything worth knowing, is ridiculously inadequate. It can affect your motivation to work by depriving you of any pleasure you might get from doing a good job, belonging to a family or being one of a group of colleagues, and from earning money and spending it on things other people would be glad to have. It can take away your ability to enjoy intimacy with those you love, isolating you socially even more than usual by making you see yourself as downright ugly instead of merely unattractive. You feel that you are a burden to others, so miserable that in the end you stop telling the truth about how you feel even to those who care most about you, because for them to understand exactly how bad your depression is they would have to be as miserable as you, and this is not something you would wish on your worst enemy.

If any of these things has happened to you – perhaps in response to a 'bad patch' which you are over now – you were badly depressed at the time, and you have had a taste of the way depressed people feel all the time. You were also very lucky to get better. If some of them happen often and you know they will happen again soon, and you feel trapped by this, then you are suffering from depression.

So is it a real 'medical' illness? If we define illness as a condition which incapacitates, debilitates, and destroys the quality of life of an individual, then there can be no alternative but to describe depression as an illness. It is a 'medical' illness in the sense that medicine can do a great deal to relieve the symptoms that depressed people experience, and in the sense that doctors in general recognize depression as an illness in its own right. And is it serious? Of course. Each person who suffers from it even for a short period is hurt and in need of help – as well as being very much at risk of accidental and self-inflicted injury – so it should be taken very seriously indeed.

DEPRESSED WITHOUT REALIZING

Another question people often ask is: Can we suffer from depression without realizing it? Certainly we can feel trapped in a series of ups and downs where the downs are intolerable and the ups are not much better, without ever saying to ourselves that we 'have depression'. There are a lot of us who try to soldier on under such circumstances, and refuse to believe that there is anything basically wrong or that we need external help. After all, many of us were brought up to feel ashamed of having to ask for help, and old habits die hard. So we try to force ourselves to deal with each separate problem as it comes and try not to think too deeply about the whole pattern of crisis and coping we are going through. Some of us get angry when we are questioned about this by well-meaning people, because we feel that we ought to be able to cope, and that we are being accused of doing something wrong when told that we are not coping.

Of course, there is a sense in which we know only too well that we feel 'depressed' in the sense of being miserable, but we can feel this way without actually labelling what is happening to us as an illness. The lonely battle can go on for weeks, months, or even years before the message gets through. It is only when we have come too close to the edge of self-annihilation often enough not to be able to go on hiding the truth from ourselves any longer, or when a good friend or a doctor tells us that we are suffering from a condition called *depression* that we begin to accept the label, and to make sense of what is happening.

Does it help you to know? Yes, because knowing you are suffering from an illness can help you take responsibility for doing something about the whole of what is happening to you instead of trying to tackle a seemingly endless sequence of problems. Sufferers have often told me about their sense of relief when they first re-cognized what they were going through, because this meant they could make more sense of it all. To some extent they could blame the illness for how they felt, instead of always thinking they were to blame, and because there must be other people with the same problem, there might be some hope of finding a cure. Until then, they had simply been too close to events to appreciate any of this.

CAN ANYTHING BE DONE?

Depression is bound to be something of a mystery to those who have never experienced it, but it is also puzzling to those who know its destructive power, either because they are sufferers themselves, or because they are intimately involved in helping sufferers. There are a host of other questions which they want answered. Is there a connection between grieving and depression, and if so, what is it? What are the causes of depression? Is it your own fault when you get depressed, or is it somebody else's or just nobody's fault? Is it due to some character defect? Can it be inherited genetically? Why are depressed people so difficult to help? These are all very important questions, and I shall discuss each one of them in due course. But the most important questions of all are: What can be done about depression – is there anything that can be done about it? Can it be cured?

To take the first question first, yes, something can be done about it. You probably already know some of the steps that can be taken. Some of them – and we shall examine these in detail in the next chapter – are medical methods of dealing with depression, in the sense that you need the help of doctors to make use of them, and also in the sense that they have been developed by applying medical science and medical logic to the problem. These ways of tackling depression can be very effective in helping to lift your mood when you feel bad; they can reduce the harmful effects of the worst aspects of the illness; they can give you a respite from the misery, and this improvement can be built upon so that you get very much better.

But can it be cured? The answer to this is also yes – but not by using the standard medical approach by itself, and not by relying upon the doctors to solve the problem for you. What we have to do if we wish to cure depression is to look beyond the present orthodox medical treatment of the illness and begin to tackle it for ourselves.

And if this sounds dangerous, or insulting to doctors, then do not be alarmed. It is no more and no less than most doctors would wish you to do. Modern medicine has many limitations and those who practise it are better placed than the rest of us to recognize them. The first thing any doctor with the time to talk about it will tell you is that medicine can often help to lessen the impact of depression; but the second thing you will be told is that medicine cannot cure it – only you can do that.

HELPING SOMEBODY

I am going to show you how, and I wish to do this without building up any false hopes, so I need to refer to the reasons why you might be reading this. If your main purpose is to help somebody else, then the important thing is not to try to aim for a cure in the middle of a depressive crisis. All that a depressed person can do at that time is just about survive, and the best way you can help is to ask whether you are needed or not, and to accept the answer you are given. Don't go too far away if you are told you are not wanted; make sure you can be reached, get on with something else, and stop worrying. If you are wanted, stay as relaxed as you can, and simply be there, by the person's side, without trying to do anything to cheer him or her up. You will probably find both of these quite difficult; being told you cannot help will probably make you feel rejected, hurt, impatient or aggressive; just 'being there' and knowing that there is nothing else you can do may also make you feel helpless and miserable and you will feel very tempted to react to this by trying to reassure the person out of his or her misery, or working too hard to be cheerful. But if, at the end of the crisis your relationship has survived, this is something to be thankful for. You will be able to do more to help between crises.

The most important thing you can do is to understand depression, what it is, how it starts, and what it does to people. And here I am going to suggest something you may find startling – that the best way of helping somebody else is to help yourself first. We each have some tendency towards depression, however slight, and this gets in the way whenever we try to help somebody with a stronger tendency. What happens is that their depression makes ours worse. So whether you see yourself as a sufferer or not, I would like you to read this book first and foremost in order to understand yourself better. It will help you help others; it will help you understand your own vulnerability to depression; it may also help you in ways which are not directly to do with depression.

HELPING YOURSELF

On the other hand, if you are depressed yourself, then you hardly need to be told that even when there is no immediate crisis, hope is still hard work – and obviously this is one of those times, or you would not be in a fit state to read this. But the fact is, depression does not have to be a permanently disabling condition which you are forced to live with for ever, a trap in which you are permanently imprisoned. We *can* fight back. We can learn enough about depression in general, and about our own particular version of it, to defeat it completely. We can begin by trying to understand it, what exactly it does to us, what precisely we do to ourselves and to other people because we are depressed, and what we personally have to do to change all this. We all have a certain amount of resistance to the truth about the illness, and it can take us a long time to realize what is involved, but sooner or later we can get ourselves together sufficiently to apply some simple and effective remedies. Of course we have to begin by wanting to get better or we never will. And we have to be honest with ourselves.

If we are honest, we have to admit that it is only when we happen to be free from a 'down' that most of us want to feel better, to live happier lives, to put an end through positive means to that miserable condition which dominates everything we do. Of course, when things have been a little better for us, most of us have tried hard to break out of the cycle of barely tolerable 'ups' and appalling 'downs'. Maybe we've tried snapping out of it, pulling ourselves together, controlling ourselves better, thinking positively and all the rest of it – and found out that none of this by itself works well enough or lasts long enough to solve the problem. Yet at the same time, we have to admit that we usually go about it haphazardly. Either we try to do too much and give up too soon, or we start off convinced that we are not going to succeed, so that we do not recognize success even when we attain it. Our most common mistake is that we fail to make the best possible use of the times when we can cope, in order to prepare for the inevitable periods when we shall not be able to.

In this book I shall show you how to save up enough of the benefit you gain in the good times to make them last longer and feel better. We can also do something for ourselves to change the impact of the 'downs'. I shall show you how to be better at predicting them, avoiding them, delaying them, and at preventing them. I shall also show you how to come out of them more quickly if you fail to prevent them. To do this you have to get to know far more about what precipitates your own particular brand of crisis; you also need some new ways of enabling the people around you to recognize what sets off your 'downs', and to help you react differently.

Depression can be defeated. Step by step you can lessen its impact on you enough to stop it dominating your life and taking priority over everything else. If you do this well enough it need never be quite the same problem again; it will be under control, not controlling you. It will be possible for you to forget you have depression for longer and longer periods, perhaps for ever – and that is almost as good as not having it. But you can do even better than this. To win the fight against depression you will eventually need to be able to neutralize its basic causes – and I shall show you how to do this too. Of course, there is no escaping the fact that none of this will be easy. You have a long, hard fight ahead of you, and some new ideas to take on board. You may also find that once you start winning you will come into conflict with other people, particularly those you are dependent upon, and want to give up again. But none of the ideas put forward in this book is so complicated that you need be put off, and even if some of them make you think hard about yourself and about the people you share your life with, it will be worth the effort.

MEDICINE

At this point we need to ask another question: What part does medicine play in all this? It is an important question for several reasons. First, the family doctor is the most obvious person to turn to for help, since, as I have said, depression is a recognized 'medical' illness, and there are certain forms of treatment which he or she can make available to you. If you are new to the subject, you are trying to help somebody else, or if you have only just begun to realize that you are depressed yourself, you will no doubt recognize your need to know about them. Secondly, if you have been depressed for a long time you will probably have seen your doctor more than once, been treated medically for the condition in various ways, and may have some misgivings about this. I meet many people who claim that medical aid has done a great deal to relieve their depression, and at least as many who say it has not helped them at all. But even if you are one of those who has been depressed for a very long time, who has tried everything and feels sceptical about the kind of help available from the doctors, it will nevertheless be useful for you to look at the orthodox medical approach just once more – either to help you make sense of why it did not work in your case, or as the next step in deciding what to do.

Yet it is certainly not a straightforward matter of simply going to the doctor, declaring that you are suffering from depression, and automatically reaping the benefit of all that modern medicine has to offer, so that you are eventually cured. As we have seen, medical practice with regard to the illness is not designed to cure it. So what is it designed to do?

Chapter Two

HOW CAN YOUR DOCTOR HELP?

THE DIAGNOSIS OF DEPRESSION

When you go to the surgery the general practitioner's first objective is to decide what is really wrong with you – you may think it is depression, when in fact something else is causing the trouble. Indeed, one good reason for going is to find out for certain. Following the traditional procedure used for all illness, the doctor starts by asking you what is wrong and noting any symptoms which are apparent. Next, you may be examined to find out generally how fit you are, and to see if there is a physical explanation for the symptoms. Only if there is no other way of accounting for them will depression be diagnosed.

As far as physical symptoms are concerned, when somebody is depressed there is likely to be a history of insomnia, and loss of appetite, lack of energy, persistent headaches, and digestive disturbances, such as bouts of flatulence, constipation, and diarrhoea. There is usually a long-term lack of interest in sex, too, for depressed men and women are equally likely to find persistent sexual advances distressing, even from a loving and skilful partner. But the most important sign of depression is that the patient looks and sounds miserable. For example, answers tend to be negative and non-committal, with phrases like 'not really', 'not much', and 'don't know' being used over and over again. The person's voice is dull and often monotonous, and facial expression tends to be fixed and unsmiling, while the eyes lack sparkle.

People who are not depressed usually gesture freely when they talk about themselves. They make eye-contact readily, and change their body position easily in the chair while they are speaking, sitting forwards one moment, and sitting back the next. They use quite large body movements – making their eyes go wider or narrowing them, frowning or smiling, nodding, shrugging, or turning their head – so as to emphasize the most important things they say, and to mark these out from the less important things. But the depressed person uses very few of these movements, and, when they are used, they all look small, indecisive, and slow, so that the whole effect is rather expressionless. There is a lack of emphasis in everything the person communicates, and there are often long, awkward pauses in the middle of sentences when it is not clear whether the speaker is still thinking or has finished what he or she has to say.

Many patients talk of a tendency to weep frequently and to feel embarrassed by their inability to control this. They may dissolve into tears in the surgery, particularly if spoken to in a kindly and sympathetic manner. Others talk of 'weeping inside' – a feeling of 'weeping in your head' but not letting people see that you are doing this, in the same way that you might want to say something nasty to somebody, and say it 'in your head' rather than out loud. They have usually been like this for a long time, and may be clever at covering up their true feelings. If so, talking to the doctor requires a great effort and quite a lot of courage on their part. Hurrying them along or interrupting them can easily cut them off altogether so they lapse into silence.

The sense of total despair and lack of interest in life is often accompanied by suicidal feelings or a strong impulse towards self-harm which falls short of actual suicide. People talk of hating themselves, and wanting to hurt their own body, about feeling utterly worthless and ashamed, or feeling constantly guilty about something. When questioned about the reasons for this, the patient is often hard put to explain. If reasons are given, the person often begins by saying things like, 'I expect you'll think it is all wrong, but . . .' or, 'It's silly, I know, but . . .' Depressed people are usually very concerned that their reactions to life make very little sense to other people.

There are often signs of extreme anxiety too – a suppressed or quite obvious feeling of panic about things other people would probably cope with fairly easily. For example, minor money worries might seem to the doctor to be blown up out of all proportion, or what appear to be slight differences of opinion with a member of the family or with a colleague are offered as proof of being hopelessly inadequate. The patient says he or she simply cannot face the future, that it is leading nowhere, or that everything is out of control and getting worse all the time. 'I know it's ridiculous, but I just can't go on like this' is a typical comment.

TREATING SYMPTOMS

People are sometimes surprised and disappointed when their doctor does not seem very interested in discussing their reasons for feeling depressed. Why does this happen? The main explanation is that the procedure used by the doctor is based on the common sense idea that the most important thing to do, whatever the illness, is to deal with the symptoms. After all, this is what most people who are ill want, and provided it is done effectively any patient should improve even if the true causes of the illness are unknown. In fact, all the standard medical treatments for depression are designed to deal with the symptoms. So once the doctor has decided that the problem is depression, he or she may act as though the causes are irrelevant. In any case, the reasons people give for feeling depressed are often things the doctor is powerless to change – such as problems at work or at home, bereavement, a recent divorce, growing older, and so on.

So you might be told in effect to go away and sort it out yourself – and there could be many reasons for this. Some doctors miss the signs of depression – they are more used to telling people what to do than to listening carefully to what they have to say, and so they simply do not notice some of the more subtle indicators of distress – the ones which only show up in the 'body language' of the patient. Some general practitioners are unable to stay detached and objective – they may be depressed too and think you should live with it as they have to. You may not explain yourself very well either, because you feel the doctor isn't being sympathetic. But the most common reason is probably that some doctors are sceptical about treating people for unhappiness, and take the view that however miserable you are, it is better for you to try to deal with it yourself than to come to rely on doctors for help.

ANTI-DEPRESSANT DRUGS

If depression is diagnosed, and the doctor decides to treat the condition, what next? One option is to prescribe a course of anti-depressant drugs. These are intended to alter the way that the nerves in your brain do their work. Research has shown that if certain chemicals are not present in sufficient quantity in the brain, mental function slows down, and the result is a flat, unresponsive mood such as that so often reported by depressed people when they are between crises and go to see the doctor. Anti-depressants are designed to make sure that there is no deficiency of these chemicals, either by stopping the brain from using them up too quickly, or by adding to the supply.

The advantage of this group of drugs is that they can lift your mood enough when you are barely able to cope for you to be able to cope more easily. The effect of all drugs varies from person to person, but in some cases the change is dramatic, and the benefits last for some time and can be built upon. Some people also feel better because they are being taken seriously by the doctor, and are 'officially' ill; perhaps they will also be treated more considerately by members of their family who were previously sceptical and impatient with them. But all anti-depressants have two main disadvantages. The first is that they cause side-effects which the doctor needs to keep an eye open for. However, drugs are improving all the time, and every new generation of them seems to be safer in this respect than the last. The second disadvantage – and to my mind the more important one – is that, as every doctor knows, drugs are not, and never can be, a cure for depression. They are strictly for the relatively short-term control of one particular symptom of depression, the flat and unresponsive mood which depressed people tend to show in the 'up' part of the cycle. The crisis itself does not go away, although 'downs' may occur less frequently and not last so long. Of course, you may decide that these disadvantages are worth putting up with compared with the full force of your depression. But if you eventually decide to come off drugs you will still have your depression, and in the meantime you may have done nothing about curing it. Some people also have quite a struggle coming off them.

Are there other drugs you might be given? You might be given sedatives – often called 'tranquillizers' – but these are really intended to treat anxiety. Taken by themselves they might dampen your mood to an even lower level, making you feel more depressed, and reducing you to something approaching a sleep-walking zombie. So a mixture of anti-depressants and tranquillizers is often used in treating depression accompanied by extreme anxiety. The different kinds of drugs have to be taken at the right time of day so that they have the desired effect.

COUNSELLING

Another option at the doctor's disposal is to listen to you and offer sympathy and understanding, but without prescribing drugs. Listening to somebody as a way of helping is called 'counselling' and the value of this has long been recognized in medicine. In recent years it has become even more popular as a way of helping people deal with emotional problems including depression. However, we need to say more about it, because there are widely differing views as to what exactly constitutes counselling, and the most helpful kind of counselling where depression is concerned is not one of the standard forms of treatment.

For many years, counselling meant listening sympathetically and giving advice. To be qualified to do this you had to be a good and wise person with a kind face and lots of first-hand experience of the problem. You might have some training, but apart from specialized areas such as marital difficulties and students' problems, most counsellors were untrained. In fact, most of them were 'dutch uncles', gentle and kindly bullies, who told you what you should do, however painful this was to hear, and sorted you out by getting you to buck up your ideas and believe in yourself a bit more. The wise old family doctor was often seen as this type of person.

Although this is still a widely held view as to what counselling is, there are now many people who see it very differently. Modern counselling helps you help yourself by enabling you to explore what you really want to do, and the counsellor is specially trained to use a whole range of skills while you do this. He or she is completely encouraging and 'on your side', and never tells you what you ought, should, or must do. As a result you can safely and confidently look in depth at your whole life and start growing again as a person not in spite of your problems, but because of them – not just making the best of the situation, but making the most of yourself. This sort of counsellor needs more than a kind face and a fund of good advice. He or she has to undertake a long and detailed training course – counsellors need to understand their own problems as well as other people's. More and more doctors are beginning to train in this way, and an increasing number of other health professionals receive limited training also. But modern counselling of this kind is still a long way from becoming a standard treatment for depression. It is time-consuming, and therefore expensive, and people who can do it are rare. The vast majority of people who offer counselling are still the old-fashioned type who will be judgemental and give you well-meaning advice – including telling you to pull yourself together and sort yourself out. Of course, if you could do this, you would already have done so. If your doctor is one of the few who really understands counselling and is trained to use the latest techniques, nevertheless he or she may not have the time to spare to help directly, and may advise you to seek counselling privately from an accredited professional.

THE TERMS DOCTORS USE

It will be useful at this point to look at some of the terms which doctors use to describe depression. One distinction which is often made is between 'reactive' and 'endogenous' depression. These may sound like two quite different illnesses, but they are not. 'Reactive' means that the doctor thinks the patient is 'reacting' to some recent event and believes this to be the immediate cause of the depression. 'Endogenous' on the other hand, means that there appears to be no immediate cause which by itself would account for the patient's misery. Another label which is sometimes used is 'clinical depression', meaning 'depression serious enough for medical treatment'. There is a growing body of medical opinion that all such labels are misleading and that all forms of depression should be taken equally seriously, whether there is a clear link with a recent event or not, whether it lasts for only a short time or has been going on for longer, and regardless of whether medical treatment is thought to be appropriate.

Another pair of words you might meet are 'psychotic' and 'neurotic'. Some patients believe in a hidden conspiracy or in a complicated, secret, and usually outlandish explanation for what is happening to them – a reality which only they understand, and which they regard as the objective truth of the matter. They would be seen as 'psychotic', or suffering from a 'psychosis'. But a 'neurosis' is an illness or quite minor hang-up in which the person who has it stays fully in touch with reality, perhaps producing unusual behaviour and over-reacting in strange ways to certain types of situation, but always aware that this will seem odd or out of proportion to other people. Depression by itself is medically classified as a neurosis and not as a psychosis; of course, people who are 'psychotic' can also suffer from depression.

REFERRAL?

Your doctor, then, has several options in undertaking to help you at the surgery – to prescribe drugs, to give you a pep-talk, or to suggest counselling. Another option is to refer you to a specialist. This will be unlikely if there is a clear reason for the unhappiness which you yourself understand, and if you are just able to cope. For example, you may feel depressed because you have recently lost your job, or become divorced or separated. You feel very miserable, but you can manage because you have support from friends and relatives. Or there may be circumstances at home which are causing problems, and you need a little help because things are getting you down. Maybe you have elderly parents to look after who are demanding and critical, a handicapped child who is placing extra strain on you and your family. Or perhaps you are young and living at home, and have had a battle with parents which has left you bruised and battered and miserable. In cases like these, the doctor will probably take the view that the unhappiness will go away quite soon of its own accord if you give it time, talk the problem over with a friend, or take a short holiday.

Of course, your unhappiness may be the result of a recent bereavement. From the doctor's point of view your distress is to be expected, so you need sympathy, reassurance and support and he or she may suggest that you visit the surgery regularly for a month or so. Loss of appetite, insomnia, and some of the misery may be relieved by drugs. In all these cases the doctor has to make sure that there is no danger of physical complications as a result of the stress, so you might be sent to the hospital to have some physical tests.

REFERRAL AS AN OUT-PATIENT

In certain cases, however, the doctor will choose to refer you to a specialist because of your depression. He or she keeps overall responsibility for the case, but hands over the treatment to a psychiatrist – a doctor specializing in psychiatric medicine at a local hospital, who can prescribe drugs, supervise treatment at the hospital, and who will have a team of specially trained ancillary workers to help. Incidentally, a 'psychologist' is quite different from this, being somebody who has studied the science of human behaviour, but who is not qualified medically and may not be at all interested in emotional illness. Some psychologists are called 'Doctor' because they have a research degree in psychology, usually a Ph.D., or 'doctorate of philosophy'. Psychologists who work with emotionally ill people in hospital are called 'clinical psychologists'.

A family doctor will probably recommend out-patient treatment if the patient can more or less cope with everyday life, but the cause of the misery is obscure, or the person's reaction seems to be 'over the top'. For example, the patient may report feeling miserable and weepy 'for no reason at all', or somebody who is grieving might seem to be taking an abnormally long time to pull through. The doctor will then arrange an appointment for a psychiatrist to interview the patient at the hospital and make a rather more detailed diagnosis. Out-patient treatment typically consists of going on to anti-depressants together with either one-to-one 'psychotherapy' or group therapy spread over a large number of visits. Psychotherapy is like the sort of modern counselling described earlier, though it might go deeper. Group therapy brings together maybe twelve patients who talk about their problems in the group and learn from this how to face up to and overcome them.

Does it help? The answer is that it helps a great deal if you are lucky in the hospital you are sent to. However, out-patient treatment can mean weeks of attending a group where you may be too shy to join in most of the time, where you feel no sense of being like the other members of the group, and where the purpose of the activity may not make sense to you. For example, depressed patients might be mixed in with psychotic or over-anxious ones – and the person in charge of the group may lack the skill to give equal attention to depressed and shy members when the psychotic or anxious ones demand more than their fair share. Where it is available (and there are many hospitals where it is not), even psychotherapy can be a mystery – you may not have a clue why you are being asked the questions that are put to you, and if you insist on straight answers to your own questions you are probably not going to get them, but might be asked instead why you are feeling aggressive. In any case, the sessions may last less than half an hour a week, with each visit ending before you feel you have got anywhere. In many hospitals there is a different clinical psychologist to see you every few visits, and it seems obvious from the questions you are asked that the last one told this one nothing about you. You have the advantages of being on anti-depressants, but you also have the disadvantages we looked at earlier.

REFERRAL AS AN IN-PATIENT

In-patient treatment will only be recommended by the family doctor as a last resort – usually because the patient's response to depression is placing that patient or his or her family in danger. For example, the patient may stop eating and lose all interest in looking after himself or herself. He or she may refuse to leave the house, become extremely withdrawn, and either make threats of suicide, or carry out a self-harming act. Neither the patient nor his or her family can cope with the crisis sufficiently to be able to lead a normal life. Under our present laws in-patient treatment is voluntary on the part of the patient, but doctors have powers under the Mental Health Act by which they can force somebody to accept hospital admission for psychiatry for a limited period in an emergency.

What does in-patient treatment for depression consist of? These days people who receive it are mainly there so they can be fed and looked after and observed whilst being treated with tranquillizers and anti-depressants. They need a great deal of help at first – to recover physically from any self-harming action that might have led to their going to hospital, to learn to look after themselves again and take an interest in life, and to adapt to, and eventually take over for themselves, the regime of medication which will control their depressive symptoms. During their stay in hospital most patients have occupational therapy, which encourages them to do various things to keep busy, to renew their interest in life, and to get their brains working again. So how long does treatment last? For technical reasons it can take quite a long time for the doctors to be certain what is the most suitable combination of drugs to use in a particular case, and obviously some patients need more help than others, but the majority of depressed patients benefit from all this in a matter of a few months, and are able to leave.

Frequently the turning point occurs when electro-convulsive therapy (ECT) is used. What happens is that the patient is first given a light anaesthetic, and then a mild convulsion by means of an electric current passed through the brain. Nobody knows why it works as well as it does – and the relief from depression which it produces may be short-lived – but it makes enough of a difference in most cases for the symptoms to be relieved, and this gain can be built upon as part of the whole treatment at the hospital. That there are worrying aspects of ECT is recognized in law: a patient can withhold consent, but the doctors have powers whereby they can override this.

Although the majority of patients leave hospital in a far better condition than when they went in, there are nevertheless several disquieting aspects of the standard forms of in-patient psychiatric treatment. The main problem is that patients are far too readily regarded as passive recipients of their treatment, as if what is being done to them is in some way none of their business – not something they should concern themselves with, but simply accept. In many hospitals this is also the way that friends and family are dealt with; they are not told how they can help, and if they try to find out they are treated as a threat to the system, so that they often end up feeling dismayed, angry, or rejected. Psychotherapy, and group therapy, which might help people understand what is wrong with them, often play no part at all in the treatment, and where they are available they are often done badly.

WHERE TO?

So where have we got to? There is no doubt that medicine can help you a great deal if you are depressed. The problem is that when you accept medical help, unless you are extraordinarily lucky, you hand over the management of your depression to people who deal only with the symptoms, and who do not or cannot help you understand why you are ill. One result is that there are a great many people who have suffered from depression for as long as they can remember, who have received treatment for it over many years, but who still have the illness. Drugs help them cope with it most but not all of the time. Another result is that there are just as many people – perhaps even more – who suffer daily as a result of depression but who receive no medical help. Sometimes this is because their doctors see no point in making them dependent on drugs for their happiness while they can apparently manage without them. Sometimes it is because the depressed person would rather soldier on without drugs than come to rely upon them. You, or the person you are concerned about, almost certainly fit into one of these categories. Whichever group you belong to, your choice lies between letting other people manage your depression on your behalf, or trying to understand it and taking charge of it for yourself. If you wish to take charge, how can you start?

Chapter Three

WHAT CAUSES DEPRESSION?

WHAT DO WE MEAN BY 'CAUSE'?

Medicine is not by itself the answer to depression. The only answer is to take charge of your own life and do something about the illness for yourself. I shall show you in detail how you can do this, but it is a good idea right now to explain what is involved. First, you need to understand what causes depression, and this is what we shall cover in this chapter and the next one. Second, you need to gain a new insight into your own version of the illness, and to commit yourself to becoming a healthier person all round, doing much of this for yourself, but also helping others to help you. The rest of the book will show you how. But the long fight to defeat depression begins with a single step – the moment when you begin to take charge of your depression for yourself because you understand what causes it and can see for yourself that you are not a helpless victim of any of these causes. Our next objective, then, is to understand more about the origins and effects of the illness.

So what do we mean when we talk about the 'causes' of depression? The problem is that we generally mean any one of three things, all of which can easily get mixed up and which we need to sort out. We can look at an example to illustrate this. Suppose we imagine a person who is depressed. We can call her Jean, and say that she is in her early forties, married, and has three children. She shows all the signs of being depressed and tells us that she has been this way for as long as she can remember although, like most depressed people, she has good days and bad days. Two years ago her mother died, and this happened just at the time that her husband changed his job and began to spend weekdays away from home, returning at weekends. Since then the relationship between Jean and her husband has deteriorated. What are the causes of her depression?

First of all, there is a set of *circumstances* which we can blame. In Jean's case this obviously includes her bereavement, and the fact that her husband is away from home most of the week. Even if they had not happened at about the same time, both these events would have upset her, making her life harder for the next year or so. The fact that they coincided means that the depressing effect of one event has been made even worse by the second. The circumstances which surround any depressed person usually work in this way – there are several reasons in the recent past for the person to feel miserable, and each one makes the others harder to bear.

For example, the combination of problems helps to explain why Jean and her husband do not get on as well now as they used to. He thinks she should cope better, and she feels very hurt because he is not there when she most needs him. Also, if we look in more detail at what has been happening lately in Jean's family, we can expect to find further repercussions. For example, her children will have been more of a problem, since they have lost their grandmother, have had to cope with a grieving mother, and at the same time have seen far less of their father. And Jean herself, now in her early forties, may feel the need to do something more with her life than be a wife and mother. This isn't easy when you have three children to look after, even if you have a husband around to help while you go out to work or to study – and hers isn't around these days. So she probably resents the fact that her own plans have had to be put on one side in favour of her husband's new job just at the time when her mother's death made her even more aware than usual that she herself wasn't getting any younger. At the same time, she cannot alter the facts: her mother has died; her husband's new job is important; and she is more than forty years old.

All this helps to explain in broad terms why Jean is going through a bad patch, and why she has felt herself to be under pressure lately. Since she cannot change the main facts of her circumstances, it also helps us to understand the feeling of being trapped which is a feature of every type of depression. Nevertheless these circumstances do not by themselves cause her worst attacks. It is not enough to say that she is 'just depressed' because her mother died and her husband works away from home all week; that would be less than the truth – just as you are not 'simply' depressed because you are overworked or out of work, because you have just had a baby, or you are short of money, or because you have suffered a bereavement.

The fact is, nobody is ever 'just depressed' because of their circumstances. After all, like Jean, we all have good days when we can cope, as well as bad days when we can't, whatever the circumstances. So we also need to look at what causes the bad days, the actual crises of depression. For example, why does Jean feel more depressed today than she felt yesterday? Why does she cope better during the week, and start to feel worse as Friday approaches, even though she has been looking forward to her husband being at home? What actually sets her off so she becomes withdrawn and weepy? To answer questions like these we need to look at a second type of cause for depression – the actual event which acts as a *'trigger'* for the attack.

Let us imagine a particular incident. All this week Jean has coped; on the Friday her husband comes in, says nothing to her, dumps his dirty washing on the kitchen floor, ignores his eldest son who wants to ask about going to a football match, and snarls at the youngest boy who then quarrels with his little sister. Next, Jean's husband disappears upstairs for a bath, using up all the hot water.

From Jean's point of view any one of these events could trigger a depressive crisis. Each by itself could make her feel that she is in a hopeless situation, surrounded by people who could not care less about her, who only need her to do the chores, but who take no notice when she does them. When all the events are added together, all she can see whether she looks at the past, the present, or ahead of her into the future, is a lifetime of wasted effort and non-recognition. Nor does she see any point in protesting out loud. She is convinced that her family would simply not understand; their behaviour right now is ample proof of this, and it did not help the last time she complained. She can see nothing good about her life, and no way out of it. She withdraws into herself and tries not to cry.

So we now have two ways of answering the question: What causes depression? First, there is a set of general circumstances which add up to a period of difficulty in our lives. Second, these circumstances increase the likelihood of our being faced at any moment with a series of insurmountable problems in quick succession, so that an attack begins. Of course, if Jean were somebody else, the triggers might not have this effect. You might think, for example, that she should hammer on the bathroom door, throw the smelly socks and soiled underpants into the bath on top of her husband, clip her second son round the ear, tell her eldest to stop whining, and then go round to the local for a double gin and a laugh about it all with the landlord. But that simply isn't Jean. She could no more react in that way than fly to the moon.

And that leads us to the third type of 'cause' – the sort of person you are. Jean, in common with all the millions of us who get depressed, has some kind of susceptibility, some in-built *vulnerability* to depression. There is a part of her physical or mental make-up that causes her to react the way she does – to respond to the triggers by feeling unable to cope, so that she enters the crisis phase of her depression. As we saw, she has been like this as long as she can remember – just about coping until she hits a particularly bad patch and then being faced with events which trigger an attack. In other words, something prevents her from reacting in any other way, and whatever this 'something' is, it adds up to the root causes of her becoming depressed. The lesson for the rest of us is that we cannot begin to defeat depression unless we first understand more about each one of these three separate kinds of cause – circumstances, triggers, and vulnerability – so the next step is to look at each type of cause in even more detail.

CIRCUMSTANCES

Most of us would have no difficulty in writing out a list of the sort of circumstances where we would expect somebody to feel seriously miserable. At the top of the list we would undoubtedly place bereavement, the death of somebody who was important to us. We can understand the misery and grief that results from the death of a husband or wife, and maybe even more so the grief of parents when a child dies. The death of a close friend or colleague can be equally devastating. We also accept that people need to mourn when they lose a parent – even where the death was expected for a long time, or if the person who died was old and cantankerous, and treated the rest of the family with contempt.

The reason why we grieve when we are bereaved is that the relationship with the dead person has been lost for ever. But the break-up of any important relationship, even where nobody dies, also causes us to grieve. When a marriage comes to an end through separation or divorce, or when we know in our hearts that it is over in all but name, we have a similar reaction. A part of us has been cut off, and we can never be the same again when this happens. We are faced with the cancelling out of all we have ever done together, with the disappointment of knowing that what we had hoped for will now never happen, and with the need to accept this loss and to build a new future for ourselves. The same applies when we lose a job we valued or, indeed, when we experience any significant loss, including the loss of part of our body or its capability through accident or surgery, permanent exile from a place we have loved, or the loss of a pet animal who has been a close and adored companion. Grief is the universal reaction to significant loss, and a natural part of grief is sorrow. This sorrow increases the likelihood of a depressive reaction.

How does this actually happen? Fortunately, we know quite a lot about grief and the way it affects us from studies of people who are grieving. There are basically three stages to grief: shock; a crisis of commitment; and the recovery phase. Our reaction to significant loss always begins with shock – the numbing of the senses that we each experience when we first guess that something dreadful has happened. This is because the body has a safety mechanism that protects us from the tidal wave of emotion that might otherwise push our heart rate and blood pressure up to a physically dangerous level. When the shock eventually wears off – and this can take a very long time – we begin to try to take in the awful truth that it really is happening to us, at first not being able to believe this, then feeling angry about it or fearful of the consequences. As our sense of loss comes home to us, however, we begin to question whether we really want to go on as before. We enter the second, or 'crisis' stage of grief.

We ask ourselves whether life is worth living any more. Is life without the one you loved and needed and depended upon worth living now that person has gone? Is it worth fighting all the battles of life to build a future, now that the future you had worked so hard for is impossible to attain? What was the point of the years of hard work, the disappointments and the triumphs now they have all come to nothing? If you had known it would end in disaster, would you have striven so hard?

Our commitment to life will be tested to its utmost during this crisis, and only if we decide to struggle on can we get through it, and go on to the recovery stage. If not, then either we become determinedly suicidal, or lapse into apathy and merely stay alive. That is to say, we are not committed to either living or to dying, and we can just about cope with existing. Recovery can only begin if we choose life and begin to face the future and our need to rebuild our shattered hopes.

But even if we choose life, for a long time afterwards we are still not safe. Recovery from grief is not a smooth, automatic progress but one which is often a case of two steps forward and then three back. Although we may be getting over the loss, anything which reminds us of it too vividly, or which threatens the small gains we have made, can send us back down again into the pit of crisis. So what often happens is that there is an additional, fourth stage in grieving – a succession of *set-backs*. Each threat to our progress seems to demonstrate once again that the life we are left with is not much better – or maybe even worse – than being dead.

TRIGGERS

If all this sounds familiar to you as a depressed person, then so it should be, for two reasons. First, depression often grows out of grief. For some reason or other some of us get stuck, unable to free ourselves from the misery, so we go from crisis to set-back and into crisis again, losing all the gains we have made, and wanting to be dead. The fact is, we can never quite reaffirm our commitment to life, for the life we have does not seem worth living. While this goes on we are not just grieving, we are depressed too.

Secondly, the series of shocks, crises, and set-backs to be found in grief is exactly the same pattern of response which those of us who are depressed without any apparent reason go through each time a crisis is triggered. It begins – as we saw in the story about Jean – with a quick succession of reminders of loss and unhappiness. As the effect accumulates, most of us feel shocked by what is happening – we go numb with disbelief, and the heart seems to skip a beat, or the body and the mind both switch off for a period of time which feels endless. There is the same swamping tidal wave of anger or of fear, and often there are successive waves of each emotion which wash over you while you feel helpless to prevent them. As you begin to realize that what you dreaded is really happening, the crisis of commitment to your own life begins again. You say to yourself that if this is all life has to offer, you might just as well not bother. There is no point in going on with the struggle any longer. You and your life are an absurd mistake, a silly nonsense, an embarrassment, an apology for an existence.

So it is easy to see why we so often confuse grief with depression. They are very similar. Both follow the same pattern – a shocking reminder of the futility of life, the overwhelming feeling that it is not worth living, and the destruction through a succession of set-backs of everything we have done recently to make ourselves feel better. But there is an important difference between the two. Grief is always a reaction to an obvious loss, but where depression is concerned there is often no obvious loss.

For you to stop coping, there need not be an obvious cause, a real loss that others can recognize and sympathize with. Of course, that might happen, but a crisis can be triggered without one. All it takes is the *threat* of such a loss. People who are not depressed find this difficult to believe – they do not see the threat the way you do, so they cannot understand why, when there has been no immediate change in your circumstances, or even when they appear to be getting better, you react just as badly as if you had recently been told about a very severe bereavement. But the threat which brings on a crisis of depression is in fact just as bad as a real loss. It has the same effect – shocking you again, making you very angry or very afraid or both, cancelling recovery, and leaving you wishing once more that you were dead or had never been born. In other words, the threat by itself is enough of a set-back to trigger the crisis of commitment to life. It acts as yet another proof, as if you needed any, that you are trapped in a life that is not worth living.

Let us use the story of Jean to illustrate what I mean. Every Friday she looks forward to her husband coming home – but when he does so on the day we looked at, he hardly talks to her, takes no responsibility for his washing, the children, or the hot water. Each of these actions might seem trivial to an outsider. But to Jean each one is a shocking reminder that she is achieving nothing with her life. Not talking to her shows her the futility of trying to be her husband's close companion and lover – something she has worked hard over the years to achieve, but is now in danger of losing because he is away all week. The way he dumped the dirty washing on the kitchen floor tells her that there is no point any more in trying to be a well-organized wife with a tidy kitchen. Moreover, she hates being treated as an unpaid servant, only there to run around after him, and in the past this has led to many fights which she has lost. Ignoring the oldest boy threatens her because she had told him to ask his father about the football match, and this has come to nothing now. She will have to start all over again trying to get her husband to take more notice of the boy – another of the 'losing battles' of her life. The way he snarled at the second child provokes a quarrel between this boy and his young sister, making Jean look like a bad mother whose children are always fighting – something she has always dreaded becoming. Using up all the hot water threatens the arrangements she had made in her head for having a bath herself so they could go out together – but here she has only herself to blame because she had said nothing about her plans. But what chance did he give her to mention this? As usual, no chance! So what is the point of even thinking about going out together?

Each little thing by itself acts as a threat to all she is by reminding her of the total hopelessness of her position in life. In fact, each threat doesn't just remind her – it rubs salt into the wound. Taken together, all the threats and the anger and fear they produce mean that Jean is so overwhelmed that she feels her position to be utterly indefensible, and her life to be totally meaningless.

The triggers which cause you to feel unable to cope any more may not be exactly the same as Jean's. But whatever they are, they all have the same effect of threatening your position in life. This is tantamount to threatening your life itself. They show you that your life consists only of losing battles, and that any gains you might have made recently are not worth keeping. You are stunned for a moment as trigger after trigger is pulled, and then react with such intense anger or fear or worry that you feel unable to struggle any longer. You are being held down in a trap you will never get out of. All this can happen in less than a second. You 'just know' that there is no point in going on.

VULNERABILITY

But why are you like this? Why is it that you react to loss in this way, whether there is an actual loss or not? Over the years experts have suggested several explanations, and we need now to take a look at them to see which is the most likely candidate.

One set of explanations comes from physiology – the science upon which modern medicine is founded, which investigates what happens inside the body. The physiologists tell us that the problem might be one of brain and nerve function – in effect, that a chemical imbalance in the brain or the nervous system is responsible, or that the hormones which carry messages to all parts of the body telling it how to react to stress may be at fault. Yet they also tell us that these chemical balances change just as much and quite naturally in perfectly healthy people as a response to external events, such as emergencies which terrify us or make us very angry.

So the body chemistry explanation is like the old 'chicken and egg' riddle. Which comes first – the external event or the chemical imbalance? Are we more likely to become depressed because our chemicals are out of order; or are the chemicals out of order because we are depressed? The physiologists cannot tell us this. The best they can say is that it could be either, and is probably a bit of both. Certain people may have abnormal brain chemistry, and some events like having a baby, or catching a virus infection, can produce changes in the hormones and enzymes affecting nerve and brain function. But the fact remains that most depressed people have perfectly normal brains, nerves, and hormones. Their bodies are not 'over-reacting' to threat. It is just that the extent of a threat as they see it is not the extent of the threat that a non-depressed person would perceive. They react to what they perceive – not to what other people think they should perceive, so to other people it will look as though they are over-reacting. The discrepancy is so great that the depressed person gives up any hope that other people will be able to see things his or her way and understand the reaction.

There is, of course, another 'body chemistry' explanation that is popular at the moment. Some people argue that our diet is to blame, and that we eat many chemicals which are bad for us – substances which are harmless to some people but to which others may be allergic. We are right to consider this; if you suspect an allergy it is a good idea to have checks to find out for sure. But it does not seem to me an adequate explanation of depression. Many people know they are allergic to certain foods but still eat them when they hit a crisis. Until there is evidence that all the millions of depressed people in the world are the victims of the food industry I shall keep an open mind but look elsewhere for the reasons why most of us get depressed.

In any case, I must admit to feeling suspicious about the 'brain chemistry' explanation of depression generally, and it is only right that I should come clean on this. It seems to me that there are powerful vested interests in getting us to believe that the causes of the illness are physiological. First, it helps to sell anti-depressants – a major money-spinner for the drug companies. Second, it helps to justify the lack of psychotherapy in hospitals, since using drugs is much cheaper in the short-term. Third, if depression is purely physiological then those in charge of treating depressed people can avoid getting mixed up in all the destructive feelings that make it such an unpleasant illness – they can stay detached and remote and 'clinical' with far less effort. Fourth, there is the vested interest of the family of the sufferer. It is often easier for them to blame a quirk of body chemistry than to undertake the painful process of re-examining their relationship with the depressed person. Finally, although drugs work by altering the chemical balance in the brain, this does not necessarily prove that the illness is caused in the first place by an imbalance of brain chemicals.

So I cannot believe that body chemicals are definitely to blame, or that this idea gives us the best explanation as to why some of us get deeply depressed, and some of us appear not to. But if this is not the explanation, then what is? One widely accepted view is that there is something in the character or the personality of the victims of depression which sets them up for their attacks. Could this explain why they seem to others to be over-reacting to threats, and why they feel unable to resolve their commitment to life? Could it explain how they get trapped in a life they do not think is worth having? We need to consider this idea next.

Chapter Four

IS IT YOUR FAULT?

CHARACTER

I have often heard it said that somebody's potential for depression is due to a 'character fault' or 'personality defect'. We have to be very careful in looking at this idea, however, because although we tend to use the words 'character' and 'personality' to mean the same thing, in fact they have two quite separate meanings and two very different histories in the world of ideas.

The idea that each person has a 'character' goes back to Victorian times. The word itself comes from the Greek for a die-stamp – something with which you can make an impression by embossing metal or paper, or like one of those signet rings with a pattern cut into it for marking the wax that letters were sealed with. For hundreds of years it had been believed by Christians that all mankind was sinful, and that this was because Eve tricked Adam, giving God no choice but to expel them both from the Garden of Eden. Logically, of course, this also meant that all babies were born full of sin. But in early Victorian times ideas began to change. For the first time in history most babies were surviving childhood, and the newly prosperous middle-class parents began to take much more responsibility for their children. This is when the modern idea of the family first became established.

At that time, people also started to reject the idea that all babies were born wicked, and began to believe instead that each child was 'innocent' at birth, with a blank and unmarked mind, exactly like soft wax. This was a revolutionary change. To the previous generation it had seemed that nothing could be done to stop children growing up to be evil. Now, however, the moral nature of the child was not a matter of chance, but became a matter of choice. A good moral character could be impressed on to the 'blank space' by the ways the parents or teachers brought up the child. As a result people began to see it as their Christian duty to control their children for 'their own good', that is to say, 'for the good of their souls'. As head of the family, the father was expected to take the main responsibility for this, and to use his considerable authority to ensure obedience in all matters of moral and spiritual significance. Mid-Victorian fathers took these duties very seriously.

But parents did not have long to ensure that their children were morally good, for as the child grew older, it was as though the wax cooled, and the young mind became much more difficult to shape. The child stopped being 'impressionable' as its character 'hardened'. By the time a child reached puberty and became sexually aware it was regarded as 'set in its ways' for the rest of its life. After that its character could not be 're-formed'.

Yet people still believed in the existence of the Devil as well as believing in God, so the idea of original sin was not abandoned, and mankind was still seen as essentially sinful. Thus, however hard you tried as a parent to bring up your children correctly, at some time between birth and puberty they could still acquire bits of wickedness which the Devil might use to tempt them into sin. These were known as 'faults' or 'failings', or as 'weaknesses'. The Victorians believed that everything a person did stemmed from the moral characteristics inside him. Good behaviour came from his virtues. Those things which went wrong in somebody's life were obviously caused by his 'faults' – in short, they were his 'own fault'.

Most of these ideas are still around. We still talk about character formation, about children being impressionable, about hardened characters, and about things being 'your own fault'. If we do not like part of our lives, we still say wryly that we have to do it 'for our sins'. The whole idea of character has been passed down from that generation to this, and many of us have accepted it without asking whether it still makes sense. But does it? How does the idea of character apply to depression?

First, it gives us a moral view of the problem. Because this whole set of ideas began as a way of preventing babies from becoming sinful, character theories have always been closely connected with morality. Those people who still stick to the Victorian view would say that if you are depressed it is because of a character fault of some kind – and this means a moral fault or weakness, in the same way that laziness or cowardice are moral faults. The idea is that the wicked or evil part of you causes you to be 'flawed' and therefore worthless or useless to others, an object of pity or contempt. Since this is 'your fault', you are supposed to feel guilty about it, but according to the theory there is nothing you can do to change it, since your character has been fixed and unalterable since the end of childhood. It might be a punishment for sins you have personally committed, or a punishment for being descended from the original sinners in the Garden of Eden. But however you have acquired your depression, because it is a moral fault or weakness, according to this view you should try to control it, and when you fail you should be ashamed of yourself. If you cannot manage this, the best you can do is to keep out of everybody else's way until you can.

Because so many of us were brought up on these moralistic Victorian ideas, I have met literally hundreds of depressed people who see their depression in this way. They not only suffer from their depression – they also make their own life very much worse by believing that it is their fault in some way and that they deserve to be depressed. Let me say now, as clearly and as forcefully as I can that nobody, absolutely nobody, 'deserves' to be depressed. Even if you have done things you are ashamed of, and deserve to be punished for them, the punishment of a life-sentence of depression is out of all proportion to your 'crimes'. No judge in the land would punish you as severely as you do yourself for any crime – including murder.

In any case, the whole idea of character is full of assumptions which are simply untrue. Take the notion that all the things you do are caused by something inside you. To the Victorians a person was lazy because he had a large piece of 'laziness' inside him. Today we know that an unwillingness to work at a task can be because there is no external incentive, and may have nothing whatever to do with what is inside the person. Or take the idea that people who lie, cheat, and steal are morally wicked. Of course they are – but it isn't solely explained by what is inside them. If you and

I were locked up in a camp, and could only stay alive by lying and stealing, we would probably do so, yet this would not mean we were liars and thieves since puberty. The external circumstances have to be taken into account to explain anything people do. You can be trapped by them through no fault of your own. But this was never understood by the Victorians.

In any case, where is this bit of you called 'laziness', or all the other evil and wicked bits which constitute your faults and moral weaknesses? In which part of the body are they to be found? If they really exist, why can't we have an operation to remove them? The fact is, they do not really exist at all as objects, or even as parts of the brain. Nor do our 'virtues' or 'strengths'. Nobody who understands anatomy today would even attempt to look for them. The whole idea is just an out-dated and unscientific explanation for human behaviour which the tide of history has left behind.

Another assumption that is part of the notion of character is that what we are is fixed at puberty, as though childhood were a kind of probationary period – our last chance to change from something potentially evil and wicked into something good and virtuous. Failing your probation means you turn into something nasty, and those nasty parts will be there for ever. This is nonsense too. First, it gives us a very distorted view of children and childhood – that there is something wrong in being a child, that as a child you are not a full person in your own right, that childlike behaviour is somehow a thing to be ashamed of. It also turns parents into people who have a moral duty and an absolute authority on behalf of the rest of society not only to control, but also to punish children 'for their own good'. Both ideas belong to the days when it was thought that children should be seen and not heard, and when the word 'childish' came to be regarded as an insult. They deprive children of their rights, and place an intolerable burden on parents. Besides, it is simply not true that what we are as adults is permanently fixed in childhood, never to change. People of any age can change.

And when does childhood end? The age at which girls have their first menstrual period is quite a good guide, but this is altering all the time. In Queen Victoria's day it happened in the late teens; today the average age is eleven and a half. No – childhood is not a chapter in our lives which can be fenced off from the rest, when we know nothing about sex and are 'innocent'. Nor does it come to a clear and definite end at a particular age so that we can put it behind us with a sigh of relief and never look back.

PERSONALITY

It is because these ideas are so full of mistakes that scientists in the early part of our century developed the notion of personality. This is a completely different way of explaining how we all turn into adults with our own individual ways of doing things, for it takes a scientific rather than a moralistic approach to what people are. It also gives us a different view of depression – one that helps us understand why it is wrong to regard it as our own fault. Above all, it helps us to see that children are people every bit as much as adults are, and that when they are disciplined and punished 'for their own good' in order to impose a certain type of character on them, they may be hurt very deeply and remain hurt for a very long time.

Today's ideas about personality have been influenced by three men in particular, the pioneers of modern psychotherapy: Sigmund Freud; Alfred Adler; and Carl Jung. Their ideas are difficult to sum up in a sentence or two, and although they worked together for several years, they did not always see eye to eye with one another. But it is fair to say that there is one thing at least on which they were all agreed – that we become who we are through a series of power struggles in early family life. The most important battles are with our parents, and these conflicts play an essential part in the way we grow up, for it is the way in which they are finally settled that determines what kind of person we become when we reach the age of independence. Freud believed they were about sex; Adler that they were about power for its own sake; and Jung that they were reflections of all the power struggles of the whole human race throughout its history. All three also agreed that we can change what we are; that by analysing our early history we can discover new ways of being ourselves and go on growing all through life.

How can the idea of personality help you with your own depression? First, it shows you where to look for the root causes of the problem – your own childhood. You developed your basic vulnerability as a result of conflict in the family you grew up in. It is part of the character that was imposed on you when you were being 'brought up', not part of your basic personality, so you do not have to take all the blame. Secondly, it shows that you can change – what has been learned can be unlearned, and you can learn not to be vulnerable to depression. In other words, damage that was done to you as a child can be undone now you are grown up. Thirdly, to tackle the problem at its roots, you need to know precisely what was done to you as a child. Finding this out can be distressing and difficult, but it is worth doing.

FAMILY LIFE

Depression is a dreadful illness – and if the root causes of it are experiences in childhood, then surely these must have been dreadful experiences. Can anything in family life be bad enough to have this effect? It hardly seems possible when you hear some people go on about the virtues of the family – the very cornerstone of civilization. In our most romantic moments we think of it as a deeply loving and caring unit, a place where people share all they have with those closest to them, which protects innocent youngsters from the harmful influences of the outside world, and where every baby is a wanted baby, and every parent is naturally good at parenthood. If families really were like this, then surely they could not be responsible for depression. But the reality is very different. There never has been such a thing as a perfect family or a perfect parent. And what is more, in many respects your own family was a very bad place for you to grow up in.

Of course, nobody is perfect, least of all parents, and there were times when what yours did to you – or to one another, so that you were affected too – was painful, or hurtful, or frightening. I accept that all parents have a difficult job to do, so perhaps it is not surprising if yours sometimes made mistakes, misused their power, and hurt you very deeply. If they did their best, then maybe you will not wish to judge them too harshly – and you may feel dreadfully disloyal even questioning their ability to care for you. But it is because of their mistakes during your childhood that you have learned to be very vulnerable to depression.

ENCOURAGING AND DISCOURAGING

So how did it happen? Most of us believe that the job of parents is to bring up their children properly – to make sure they grow up into the right kind of people. The ideal way to do this is to *encourage* children – helping them to turn into the sort of people the rest of the world needs by giving careful and loving guidance, and providing a joyful and enriching environment where life is real and often very challenging but mostly fun too. It means enabling children to experiment with being independent, helping them to take risks confidently, even if there are times when the parents feel afraid for them or disagree with their own child's values. It means rewarding them when they are successful, and assisting them to accept failure and learn from it when things do not work out for them. And it does not mean manipulating them; it means being open and honest with them. But we have to be realistic. This is not always possible.

It is only when a child is truly loved by a parent who is really enjoying life that the child can be encouraged in this way. In some families this happens often; in others it is a rare event, or one that never takes place at all.

Those of us who suffer from depression today are likely to have been more often *discouraged* than encouraged by our parents when we were little. Why do parents discourage their children? One reason is that it has long been seen as part of the parent's job to hurt a child deliberately in order to stop it turning into the 'wrong' kind of person. But what is this kind of person? To most parents it means the sort of person they do not like. For example, a parent who does not like lazy people will not want its child to become a lazy person; parents who say they can't stand selfish or inconsiderate people will try to stop a child of theirs from turning into one; good competitors want to stop their kids growing into poor competitors or bad losers; shy parents who dislike people who show off will try to stop their child becoming a show-off who embarrasses them, and so on. Notice that these controls are negative – they are all about saying no! And the irony is that very often the kinds of people that parents cannot stand are exactly the sort they are most afraid of becoming themselves – yet could easily turn into. This makes their task even harder, and to discourage the sort of behaviour which they do not approve of, they use all the power they have. Each time they disapprove of the child's actions they go out of their way to make it feel bad about what it is doing, and they keep on until it stops. And that isn't all.

SELF-CONTROL

At the same time they want to teach the child to do the 'right' thing every time without having to be told – in other words they want him or her to be somebody 'well-behaved' and 'self' controlled. But the change does not usually happen without a struggle. There are often long and difficult battles to be fought, which the parent is determined to win. I'm sure you know the sort of things parents say during these battles: 'How many times do I have to tell you?' they grumble; 'You should know that by now!' Or, 'I shan't tell you again. You can go to your room without any supper and stay there until you have learned the right way to behave.' Or, 'Your father and I are sick and tired of telling you. Please stop behaving like that – we've asked you time and time again, but you deliberately set out to hurt us!'

All the power and ingenuity of the parent might have to be brought to bear over and over again before the child gives in and learns its lesson. How often have you heard parents say that with young Bobby or Sheila, only the most severe discouragement seems to do the trick? Your own parents may have said this about you; or you heard them say it about a brother or sister, and you knew full well that this would happen to you as well unless you watched your step. Many of us can remember vividly at least one power struggle we had with a parent – or one which more directly involved another member of the family. We can never forget the 'atmosphere' this created.

CRISIS CONTROL

But the most significant discouragement which parents use is seldom the result of a carefully calculated and rational policy. Parents control their children when they themselves cannot cope and the child seems to be making things worse, either on purpose or unintentionally. It is easy enough to imagine the sort of thing I mean. Sometimes a crisis blows up out of nothing. Mum is trying to feed the baby just as the phone rings. In the middle of this the milkman knocks at the door hoping to be paid, the cat starts howling, the spuds boil over, and the toddler picks that very moment to play with the electric wires at the back of the television set. Under these circumstances the toddler is quite likely to come in for an extra bit of control. And it will be the sort that discourages, not the sort that encourages.

All parents have moments like this when they cannot cope. They are stretched beyond the limit, and as a result win a little bit of leeway for themselves by controlling the child whom they see as being a nuisance. Surely this does no great harm, and the parent who goes too far can usually put things right when he or she calms down. Unfortunately, however, this is not always what happens. The parent loses control, hits out, and forgets about it – because he or she is going through a bad patch temporarily, or may simply not know how to apologize to a child and make things right again. Or it happens because the bad patch never seems to end. Many parents are faced with insurmountable problems nearly all the time; indeed, there are many people for whom married life is one endless succession of impossible problems. In our own generation, with divorce affecting one in three marriages, this is something we can accept as normal. But we are no worse at being married than our parents were – marriage was always like this. Whether we like it or not, many of us grew up with parents who stayed together not because they were happy, but 'for the sake of the children', or because in their day divorce was harder to accept or to obtain, where today they would have split up. We were in the way in crisis after crisis – one of the reasons why they could not cope – however much they wanted us when times were good. And they made sure we knew it.

SPELLING IT OUT

What is the connection between all this, and the three kinds of causes we looked at earlier – your vulnerability, the triggers you respond to, and the circumstances within which depression occurs?

Firstly, your own *vulnerability* to depression came about because your parents went to a great deal of trouble to turn you into the kind of person they wanted you to be. They did this by 'character building' – by imposing a new set of characteristics on to your basic personality, the person you really are inside. Unfortunately, however, they went about this the wrong way, by threatening and hurting you, instead of encouraging you to be yourself. You were never told by your parents that they were doing the wrong things – either they did not know this or could not admit it. So instead of putting things right when they hurt you, they made matters worse; they said you were wrong, and they used all the power and ingenuity at their command to force you to accept this. The effect was that you were discouraged from being your true self, taught to have no faith in the essential worth of your own personality. Your faith has still not recovered.

But it also helps to explain the *trigger* system. You see, in order to make sure you would not need to be told every single time they wanted to correct or discourage you, your parents taught you to recognize situations where you had to discourage yourself and save them the trouble. They gave out very clear signals every time such circumstances occurred – threats that reminded you that they had all the power, telling you plainly that you would lose if it came to a fight with them again. These signals still work. To this day you only have to receive the right kind of threat – the 'triggers' of depression – and you 'automatically' become discouraged again. As we saw in the story about Jean, you recognize that you are once more caught up in a 'losing battle'. So you give in. You save everybody else the trouble of hurting you by hurting yourself – in effect, what you once did for your parents, you now do for the rest of the world. You either attack yourself for being wrong, withdraw so you do not embarrass other people, or feel very distressed because you think all their problems are your fault. The triggers were placed there in childhood, and you still have them. So even though you sometimes begin to accept that you are a good, valuable, lovable person at heart, as soon as one of these threats appears, you begin to doubt yourself and have a set-back.

What about the *circumstances* of depression – events such as bereavements, relationship difficulties, problems at work, and so on? If you are depressed, I am sure you will agree that these events can happen to anybody. But the fact is, you seem to get more than your fair share. Why is this? One answer is that because you are discouraged, when such things happen it takes you longer to get over the grief and sorrow than it would do if you had been encouraged as a youngster. Your grieving is full of set-backs: each new blow hits you before you have recovered from the last, and every new experience of loss makes the last one even harder to deal with. But this is only part of the truth. We live in a competitive and largely uncaring world, and the discouraged child has to fight with one hand tied behind its back. The encouraged people get the best pickings. They have the confidence to bounce back from a set-back, and get better exam grades, more encouragement to go on to college, better jobs. They get more help all round. They choose life-partners who were also encouraged by their families, and who are good at bouncing back in adversity. Depressed people, through no fault of their own, often find at thirty or forty or fifty that they are trapped in second-best lives with partners they do not really like. They marry people who have just as many problems as themselves, and cannot help them much in a crisis. Each new experience of loss turns an unhappy life into an intolerable one.

But why you? Why were you a victim when others were not? Nobody really knows, but part of the answer lies in the fact that some families are much more likely to produce discouraged and depressed children than others. Where one or both parents is depressed this is almost certainly going to be the case. It has been known for a long time that there is a strong statistical connection between being depressed as an adult and having at least one parent who suffered from depression, so much so that some scientists think the illness may be passed on in the parents' genes, although there is no corroborative evidence for this view.

What is obvious is that if you are the child of depressed parents, you must have run a greater risk of becoming the victim of discouragement. Maybe you've never thought about it before, but there is big chance that one or both of your parents suffered from depression at some time or other while you were a child. It might have been the immediate effect of a bereavement, a stillbirth or cot death, or a wartime loss. It could be connected with an attack of post-natal depression, or with some kind of illness which went un-treated due to the prevailing social conditions of the day. Or it might have been one of the consequences of a general unhappiness in the marriage, or the aftermath of a discovered extra-marital affair. There could be any number of reasons, and if you think back, or ask the right people, you may be able to identify them. But even if you know of no evidence to support this explanation, remember that those who become depressed often hide the reasons, particularly from their children, or manage to forget about them. If your parents did not enjoy life or feel confident about parenthood they may never have talked about this, but they were probably depressed, and could not encourage you.

If it is any comfort to you, then, your own depression was almost certainly caused originally by theirs, or by their own parents' depression. It could go back a very long way. You can tell yourself that they could not help this any more than their own parents could. But the fact remains that you have a choice they did not have or did not take. You can take the responsibility for doing something about the problem, dealing with the circumstances, the triggers, and your own vulnerability, and you may be the first person in several generations of your family to do so. I hope you will.

Chapter Five

WHAT IS YOUR KIND OF DEPRESSION?

Children who are more deeply discouraged than encouraged by their parents grow into adults who are seriously vulnerable to depression; they respond to certain kinds of threat by feeling very distressed, by being convinced that there is no point in fighting back, and by not wanting to go on with their life. This is what keeps happening to you. But all depression isn't exactly the same. Everybody is different; each of us responds more to some types of threat than to others, and have our own individual ways of being 'down'. From this point onwards, I am going to show you how you can do something positive about your depression, but you need to tackle your own version of it – not somebody else's. So over the next few chapters we are going to look at the many varieties of depression, and find the answers to three questions: How can you recognize the type of depression you have? What happened to you to give you this particular variety? What is it that triggers your crises today?

Let me begin with an analogy. Suppose you go into one of those fashionable new restaurants that always seem to have a gimmick of some kind, and look at the menu. At this particular place there are only three items which you can choose from: say, potato, cheese, and meat. It sounds like a rather strange restaurant, one where there really isn't much choice – but there may be more choice than you think.

One thing you could do is to pick out just one of the three items for your meal. This would give you a choice of three completely different meals. Or you might choose two of the items, and have a two-course meal. This adds up to another three choices, making a total of six. However, if you pick more than one item, you can also decide which one to begin your meal with. For example, if you decide upon potato and cheese, you could either have the potato as a first course, or have it after the cheese. Or you could opt for meat and cheese, or potato and meat, and decide which of the two you would like to start your meal with – that will give you the choice of three more meals, so now we have nine. And then there is nothing to stop you having all three of the items – in any order you want. So it is rather complicated after all. Even with only three items on the menu and freedom of choice about the order you eat them in, there is a total of fifteen combinations. And that isn't the end of the matter either. There are innumerable types of potato, cheese, and meat, and lots of ways of cooking them. For example, your potato could be either a white variety or a red one, and it could be baked, roasted, boiled, chipped, or fried. With a menu that is limited to no more than three items, you could still order hundreds of different meals.

What has this to do with depression? Surprising though it may seem, there are only three main types of depression – three ways of being vulnerable, three kinds of triggers, three sorts of things we do to ourselves during a crisis, and three ways of feeling bad when there is no crisis. In your own case, you might have only one of these reactions – just as in the imaginary restaurant you might choose just one item from the menu. But your kind of depression might mean having two of the three reactions, or all three of them –and in any order. Also, each of the three reactions has several variations. So although depression can occur in hundreds of different ways, each individual's responses can be traced back to three main elements. We can use this idea to help you identify your own version of the illness.

So what are the three items on the 'depression menu'? My names for them are: 'self-violence', 'self-banishment', and 'self-sacrifice'. First we need to get a broad idea of what is involved, and then consider each of them in much more detail so you can identify your own response pattern. But take your time as you go through them – you may find some of it distressing. If you begin to feel upset by it, just put the book to one side and come back to it as soon as you feel a bit better. The three reactions are:

SELF-VIOLENCE: this consists of the use of violence or the threat of violence, directed either at yourself or at some object. The violence can be physical or verbal or both.

SELF-BANISHMENT: this involves banishing yourself from the scene either by withdrawing physically, or withdrawing into yourself, or feeling self-conscious.

SELF-SACRIFICE: this consists of making sacrifices because you feel unlovable and a burden to other people, or because you are convinced they would be better off without you.

Each of these reactions varies from person to person, and from time to time in the same person. It also varies according to how intensely it is felt and expressed, how long it lasts, and whether or not it is acted upon physically. Quite often the reaction is felt internally without being acted upon – that is to say, you 'do it in your head'.

SELF-VIOLENCE

There are, of course, many kinds of violence, but the kind I am thinking of here is the sort of physical or verbal attack which many depressed people make upon themselves when they go into a crisis. The actual attack may be carried out, or the impulse to do it may be suppressed so that you stop yourself doing it.

A physical attack might mean that you hit yourself with your hand – the usual places being the head, the throat, the arms or legs, or the trunk. You might slap, prod, or punch. It could also mean kicking yourself, or hurting yourself by banging your head, hand, foot, or some other part of your body against a hard or sharp object. The feeling when you do this is of being almost impervious to the pain unless you do it over and over again, so you get more violent each time until you become exhausted. You might feel self-violent for hours, with the feeling coming and going in waves, or only for a relatively short time.

Some people have a strong impulse to pick up an object and cut, jab, or beat themselves with it, to damage the body physically, perhaps cutting offending parts off or beating it severely. Others feel impelled to choke the life out of it or break its neck, or have an almost irresistible urge to smash the body by throwing it from a high place; to put it in a car and drive into a wall; to hurl it under a train or a lorry. We often have an image when we feel this way of our bodies cut to ribbons, broken or bleeding, or of our brains splattered everywhere. Yes, it is distressing and painful to read such things. But many of us really do feel this way, even though, fortunately, we usually manage to stop ourselves from acting on the whole of the impulse.

In a verbal attack, what you do is call yourself names. Of course, this can be done in a very mild way – many people give themselves a gentle ticking off when they have done something careless or stupid. But at the peak of a crisis very depressed people who use this method are anything but gentle. They pour scorn on every aspect of themselves, denigrating everything they have ever done, and ever will do. Many use the foulest language they can, and shout and rave, with not only their tone of voice but every other way they have of expressing themselves completely given over to violent self-hatred. Quite often, too, this is accompanied by some kind of physical self-attack.

The third main type of self-violence consists of breaking, or threatening to break, objects. The urge you get is to smash, cut, or otherwise destroy them. Sometimes we choose the object nearest to us; sometimes it is an object which we have to go and fetch. The object itself is often one we value highly, or which was expensive, or which we have made ourselves, but it need not be something which matters to us – some people nearly always pick on a worthless object, or one that is easy to repair. Also, breaking things may take the form of throwing the contents of an object all over the place –the food from a dish or plate, the drink from a cup or a glass, the paint from a paint tin, papers or clothes from a drawer – or violently sweeping all the things from off a table or desk or shelf. Objects may be banged or rattled too – such as doors which are slammed, or pots and pans which are crashed violently. Again, we may not carry out such attacks – we may do them in our head or threaten to do them – often with violent words or gestures.

SELF-BANISHMENT

The second kind of depressive response is self-banishment. The urge to banish yourself from the scene when a crisis is triggered is one which many depressed people have. It can pass quickly or slowly, but at its worst it is an intensely experienced and highly self-destructive urge. There are many ways in which it can be expressed – for example, it may be acted upon so that others can see it, or it may be kept hidden from other people. Self-banishment might mean removing yourself physically from the scene of the threat. Some people just walk away and keep on walking. Some run away. They may not go anywhere in particular – that is to say they just walk or run away aimlessly. They are banishing themselves into nowhere, beyond the edge of everything into the unknown region where nothing exists, and where nobody will see them. If you do this, and people speak to you whilst you are there you will probably ignore them, and behave as though you yourself are not there. But it isn't everybody who banishes himself or herself into Outer Space – some of us have special places which we always use, such as a bedroom, a shed or outhouse, the car, or the garage. We might leave the door open so we can be seen, or we might lock ourselves in. A lot of people banish themselves into the bathroom. Whichever place you choose, this sort of reaction often involves curling yourself up into the smallest possible space, or choosing the dirtiest, most humiliating spot you can find. Some of us, for example, when we lock ourselves in the bathroom, squeeze up as close as we can to the lavatory.

A second way of not being somewhere you find threatening is not to go there in the first place – such as not going into a room where you know you will feel bad, not going to work, not going to see somebody, not going to a party, not going out, not going anywhere where you might enjoy yourself. You can spend your life 'not going' to places.

It is possible to banish yourself without moving; indeed, when they go into crisis this is what many people do. They don't run or walk away, they remain where they happen to be and switch off completely, perhaps standing like a statue, or just sitting or lying there, not reacting to anything that is said or to anything else which is going on around them. The feeling when we do this is of being aware of what is happening, and yet impervious to it – in much the same way that self-violence can make you feel impervious to the pain you inflict upon yourself.

The most extreme and distressing version of this impulse is to wish to stop being a body with a live person in it, and to try to become an empty shell – a body with nobody living inside it. You do not particularly want to damage the body – unless this is necessary to empty it of its tenant – just to get out and leave it there. This is the way some people feel when they are thinking about taking an overdose or of gassing or drowning themselves. Again, we might threaten out loud to do this, although many of us often have this kind of urge without ever acting upon it. Some of us don't talk about it either, or, when we mention it we try to disguise what we feel, either by joking about it or denying that we feel it strongly. Sometimes we may not even want to admit to ourselves that we feel this way. Nevertheless, there are millions of people who do, and most of them have so far never acted on it.

The third main variation of the self-banishment reaction consists of extreme embarrassment or shame, the feeling that you are utterly and totally ridiculous. Shy people who are depressed will recognize this reaction very well, although you don't have to be shy to experience it. You shrink inwardly, and become acutely self-conscious, and feel desperately afraid that your bowels will betray you. Other parts of your body might draw attention to you too – your hands, which you see as coarse and ugly, for example, or your breasts, which may utterly shame you by being too big, or humiliate you by being too small. Your nose or ears might get noticed and laughed at, or your whole body might give you away by blushing all over or smelling very bad so that other people are bound to notice that you cannot control it adequately. Your voice – its tone or your accent or the ignorance you show when you run out of words – might also attract attention so that everybody will see just how ridiculous and unaccomplished you are. Then there are your clothes – however carefully you have chosen them, they seem shabby or old, or too garish and unfashionable, or they fail to hide your skinny frame or your nasty plumpness. Sometimes certain topics of conversation turn you into an embarrassment because of how you react – a dirty joke, references to religion or politics, criticism of a person you know, or anything which sounds far cleverer than you feel you could ever be, or so stupid that you wish you were not there at all. And certain people can make you feel embarrassed or ashamed just by being there, especially those popular, attractive, and confident people who seem to have everything but really have nothing, the embarrassing know-alls or the showy bullies who take in everybody else, but who do not fool you.

SELF-SACRIFICE

The kind of crisis I call 'self-sacrifice' makes you feel you are being such a nuisance to the people around you, or that you are so utterly sorry and ashamed for all the hurt you have caused by being selfish or ungrateful, that you simply cannot go on. Of course, lots of people feel sorry for hurting somebody and wish to make amends, but there is usually an obvious and specific reason for this, and they do not feel bad about it nearly as often, nor for so long, nor as intensely as somebody facing a depressive crisis. At its most dangerous, you become convinced that the only way to make amends is for the world to be rid of you, so you will not be a problem to others ever again. In this mood it can seem a kindness to your family and friends to end your own life.

Most people who have this reaction feel a deep sense of shame at being angry or frustrated, fearful or helpless, and this leads to an almost uncontrollable urge to weep. There are people who cry out loud in anguish, hoping that somebody will hear them and come to their rescue. But most try hard not to cry in case this makes things worse, so it all goes on inside you, becoming an internal bleeding that leaves you drained of life, turning you into a pitiful heap of misery that longs to be picked up and cuddled but dares not ask for this consolation. When you feel like this you desperately hope that nobody will be kind to you, especially a stranger – you can keep the hurt inside that way. People who are casually kind to you make you lose control, so you have to tackle the painful process of putting yourself together all over again when they've gone away and forgotten you.

The events leading up to a self-sacrifice crisis can vary. Perhaps there has been a specific incident for which you blame yourself – somebody has been hurt, and it is all your fault. Or you might be worried in case somebody gets hurt because of you. Maybe you are overwhelmed by a feeling of being sorry for no apparent reason, desperate for forgiveness even though you cannot think what you did wrong. Any one of these events can produce an all-consuming feeling of having committed an unpardonable offence so that your body is racked with inconceivable tortures and your strength reduced to that of a baby.

'Self-sacrifice' often means wearing yourself out in the service of others and feeling miserable and unloved when they take you for granted. You spend your life doing your best for other people, working like a slave on behalf of your husband or wife, your children, your own parents or in-laws, a sick neighbour, the customers or your boss or colleagues at work. You know that you are doing far more than you need, and that you are often doing things for them that they have not asked you to do, but you just want to be helpful. In return you put up with their foul moods and tantrums, show endless patience when they are ill, clean up after them, fetch and carry for them. And they never even notice! Sometimes you think you shouldn't put up with all this, but say to yourself: if I didn't do these jobs, who would? And if they weren't done there would be chaos. In any case you feel guilty whenever you could have helped somebody but failed to do so. You also tell yourself that you do not want gratitude, yet you often feel really hurt when the gratitude you 'did not expect' does not appear. The weariness of endless self-sacrifice builds up until you find yourself exhausted and unable to stop weeping.

The need to do things for others and 'not expect' gratitude in return can also come out as an overwhelming need to *give* gratitude. You find yourself thanking people out of all proportion for small favours of the kind anybody would do, so that they become embarrassed. Or you might go over the top with expressions of sympathy when people mention something bad that has happened to them. You feel so sorry for them that you appear to be taking the blame for sadnesses you could not possibly have caused.

Another common part of the self-sacrifice reaction is a need to obtain permission for everything; you cannot please yourself for fear of upsetting somebody or getting people into trouble. For example, you might try to do nothing that will cause trouble, yet this gets more and more difficult until you simply don't know what to do for the best. You might keep asking somebody if he minds you doing something, then listen very carefully in case he says he doesn't mind, but sounds as though really he does. You might also 'get stuck' with people – popping in for a moment to see them and finding you cannot get away, or being unable to end mournful conversations with sad strangers. Somehow you do not have permission to get on with your own life as long as somebody else needs you. You may also find that you spend most of your time waiting for somebody who matters to get round to contacting you. You make arrangements which seem precise to you but vague to the other person – and show enormous patience and understanding when the inevitable lame excuses are trotted out. When you are hurt by people, however badly, you usually end up doing the apologizing.

How are we to make sense of all the many varieties of the 'self-sacrifice' reaction? Firstly, they all have in common a desperate need to be forgiven for being a nuisance; to say sorry for being a problem; to be grateful for small favours, or to do things without being thanked; or to say please and excuse me before you can have any life of your own. Secondly, all of them mean that you put other people's interests before your own, sacrificing your time, your pride, even your own life in an effort to please them and to avoid being selfish.

MIXTURES AND SEQUENCES

So far I have only sketched out some of the main variations of each type of crisis response. There are many more ways of having them, and some of them will become evident later when the origins of them have been explained. But I hope I have said enough at this stage for you to identify some of your own crisis responses, and to begin to work out whether you use mainly one type, two of them, or all three. You may also have been able to identify the sequences which you use. For example, there are quite a lot of people who begin with the self-violence reaction, and then switch to self-sacrifice one. First they 'tell themselves off', and then feel very sorry about this and weep heart-brokenly for forgiveness. In our story about Jean, the reaction she used was self-banishment and self-sacrifice, another commonly encountered pattern. First she retreated inside herself, and then, when she had done this, she cried 'in her head', sobbing her heart out where nobody could see or hear her to avoid causing even more trouble.

However, a word of caution is in order – if your own crisis reactions belong firmly to one category, you may feel completely unable to make sense of the rest. Thus, people who are self-violent or self-sacrificing may be mystified by self-banishment, and those who are only self-banishing may have a very difficult time understanding and being sympathetic towards the self-violent or the self-sacrifice reaction. What really matters is that you see your own kind of response somewhere on the list, or at least, enough examples of each type for you to know where it would go if I have apparently left it out. Incidentally it is quite a good idea to get out a bit of paper and a pen and write down a description of your own habitual crisis patterns stage by stage – get somebody who knows you well to help you. If you are able to do this, keep it handy – it will be useful later on.

Each of the three kinds of response is best dealt with in a slightly different way. This is because it is a different kind of statement about the sort of person you are and what you want from life, and it also says something important about what threatens you and why you feel threatened. If you know where it comes from – and, in the next chapter, I shall help you to find out – you will be able to see much more clearly what you can do about it.

But I must again stress that discovering why you react in such ways can be upsetting. It may re-awaken sad and painful memories, things you have tried to forget, and perhaps succeeded in forgetting. Your mind may defend itself from this danger by persuading you to regard the whole idea as useless nonsense, too complicated, or as a waste of time. Please, take the risk of reading the next chapter now, and finding out where your reactions came from. If you start to feel impatient, sceptical, or miserable, just give yourself more time. Remember that the things which were done to you in your childhood make you respond like this, and that your childhood is over now. You have survived. However, if you bottle up the feelings that were once used to train you, they will go on working inside you, making you miserable, and trapping you in a life of depression which you have never deserved.

Chapter Six

HOW DID YOU LEARN TO BE DEPRESSED?

HARD TO BELIEVE

There is a disturbing and shocking truth about depression which I can only state bluntly, and which you may already have noticed. It concerns the connection between your own depression and your parents' treatment of you when you where a child. The truth is that what you want to do to yourself at the worst moments of your depression is exactly what your parents *threatened* you with in order to discourage you during childhood. If you are self-violent, then actual or threatened violence was used to discourage you; if you are a self-banisher, then as a child you were discouraged by banishment or threat of banishment; if you are self-sacrificing, then you were dishonestly manipulated into making endless recompense for the harm you had apparently done to your own parents. Whatever pattern of depression you have, it began as your parents' pattern of discouragement. If you use a mixture of methods, then so did they. Above all, the more completely destructive you feel at the height of a crisis, the more certain it is that in childhood they convinced you that they would completely destroy you if you continued to displease them.

For some of us this is a very hard truth to accept. It can seem inconceivable that our own parents could have behaved in such a monstrous fashion towards a helpless child all those years ago, and that we might still be paying the price for this abuse of power. We have been told all our lives that depression is nobody's fault but our own, that it is either an accident of nature, a freak variation in brain chemistry with which we were unaccountably stricken, some lack in our personality, or some awkwardness or arrogance built into our character because we were born perverse or wicked. To be told now that what is wrong with us goes back all the way to deliberate cruelty towards us by our own parents when we were little contradicts all we have ever been allowed to think. It is far from easy for us to take on board the fact that we might have been beaten up viciously – that our parents were even capable of this; or that we were not wanted, and that at least one of our parents may have regretted or resented our presence on this earth almost from the time we were conceived until the present day; that they could have been so dishonest as to blackmail us into submission time and time again with the cruel lie that all their troubles were the result of acts of deliberate selfishness on our part. Seeing one's parents for the very first time as real, fallible people, just as capable as any other member of the human race of cruelty and injustice is one of the most difficult steps to take in life. It is also the last one which most parents would allow their own children to take knowingly. Yet we cannot be fully adult until we see through the lie of parental perfection, and reject the propaganda of perfect parental love.

If you wish to understand why you get so depressed, this set of truths cannot be avoided. And let me repeat. You are safe now from the worst your parents threatened to do: they can never again carry out their threats, and you have survived childhood with a chance of building a new future, a future for yourself, and, if you wish, for the rest of us who need you. Stay alive. Accept your survival any way you can – as a gift you deserve in compensation for the pain; or as a reward for having the courage never to have quite given in; as evidence of the indomitable spirit of mankind; or as a bit of luck that has come your way. You are safe now, so let yourself start to feel safe, one step at a time, little by little, like learning to walk again. Try to aim at beginning to feel safe enough to accept the facts of what your parents did to you, so you can start to learn how to deal with the feelings of anger and fear and sorrow which you have been left with. That is the only way you can ever begin to learn how to be your true self, to value your own personality, and to counteract your parents' need to turn you into somebody who is depressed so they could cope with you despite their own depression.

But you will also need a new perspective – a new way of looking at what was done that allows you to see that it was no more and no less than the way millions of parents behave towards children. What was done to you was unique only in the sense that you experienced a unique formula of control, but this formula was made up of elements which are common to all control systems in our society. The thought may never have occurred to you before, but the effective control of adults is only possible because people learn as children to respond to control from their parents. To help you get things into perspective we shall now look at the three main elements of control, and see which ones your own parents used on you.

'SQUASHING'

The use of violence to control children is common throughout the West, although physical violence directed at young people was probably even more common when your parents were children than it is today. This type of control is called 'squashing'. It can take the form of hitting the child; it can also mean threatening to do so using intimidatory 'body language'; it also includes verbal abuse. Obviously, the number of times per day, the degree of severity, the amount of ceremony used, and the reasons for adopting this kind of control vary widely between families. Many parents never hit their children, although two or three are beaten to death by their mother or father every week in Britain. Between these extremes there are many degrees of severity.

A child can also be 'squashed' indirectly. This is what happens when the child watches or hears somebody else being beaten up, threatened, or verbally abused – a parent, for example, a brother or sister, or even a neighbour. The same effect can also be produced when a parent threatens to break something, or actually breaks it as a way of showing disapproval. When a parent is angry, doors can be slammed most eloquently. The crashing of pots and pans from a kitchen is worth a thousand words. Even a cup banged into a saucer can speak volumes. Each of these events shows that the angry parent is in a bad mood, and each one helps to build up an 'atmosphere' of violence in the home while the bad mood lasts, so that everybody else controls his or her own behaviour for fear of making matters worse.

If you are self-violent when you hit a 'down', then the squashing method of control was used on you. You may already have recognized this. For example, if you are very violent with yourself during a depressive crisis, then you are almost certainly well aware that at least one of your parents was capable of being this violent with you when you were a child, although it is probable that the very worst violence to which you were subjected or with which you were threatened lies buried in your deep memory where you cannot reach it without risking a recurrence of the pain and fear and anger that it caused. Where you hit yourself now was where they threatened to hit you then.

If you use verbal abuse on yourself a lot during a 'down', then it is very likely that as a child you were shouted at, criticized for each little thing you did wrong, or told in no uncertain terms many times that you were stupid or careless or no good. What you tell yourself now is what you were being told then. But if you break objects, or feel the urge to do so, then you are the victim of indirect violence – you were intimidated as a child by the banging of doors, the crashing of pots, by other people being 'beaten up', by the 'atmosphere' such actions created and sustained. Of course, all three might have been used – physical, verbal, and indirect violence.

On the other hand, even though you are self-violent, you may still be puzzled by all this. Perhaps you feel that although your parents were strict, you were never placed in fear of your life – certainly not enough to feel now that sometimes you want to smash your own body. But if so, it is because you are looking back with adult eyes on the very different experience of a child. A furious, violent, and attacking parent, particularly one out of control who does not know his or her own strength, is a terrifying sight when you are little. Don't forget that you were threatened not with the amount of violence that was actually used – but with the degree of violence you *thought* might be used. A child who is being threatened has no reason to believe that the threat won't be carried out. Indeed, parents know very well that the method will not work unless they make it appear that they will stop at nothing to get their own way.

Every discouraged child learns not to wait and find out whether the parent's bark is worse than his or her bite – the child assumes the worst, because that is the only safe and intelligent thing to do. This is why depressed people always assume the worst when threatened, and why what *might* have happened is always worse for them than what actually does. It is why the threat is enough to provoke a damaging crisis. They use the amount of control on themselves which they expected their parents to use –not necessarily what really happened, but what they knew *might* happen.

If this was one of the control methods your parents used, then part of your personality will have been 'squashed'. Squashed people are typically lacking in self-confidence – and feel very critical of everything they do. Failure is the worst crime, but even when they succeed they are reluctant to accept this and would rather say that something is 'not bad' than admit that it is good. They often seem not to know their own strength, and seldom recognize how hard they are on themselves.

'IGNORING'

The second method of control used by parents is what I call 'ignoring', and consists of the banishment of the child, either from territory – such as the room where the parent happens to be – or from attention. An example of territorial banishment is being sent to your room; an example of being banished from attention is not being spoken to, listened to, or touched. In one version of 'ignoring', the child is promised something, but the reward is withheld as a punishment or simply forgotten – excluding the child from the attention it had been led to expect. 'Ignoring' controls can be fatal. At one extreme, two or three children are killed by neglect each week – locked up in bedrooms, sheds or cellars, and starved to death, or habitually left behind in houses where fatal accidents eventually happen. Some are provided for materially, but never cuddled, comforted or caressed. At the other extreme, a child may only be ignored for a short time when the parent has no other choice. Between the ends of the spectrum there are many degrees of severity.

Sometimes the parent doesn't ignore the whole of the child,

but just ignores certain of its needs, or certain parts of its body. This discourages the child from satisfying those needs, or feeling proud of those parts of its body. For example, many parents deliberately ignore their child's sexuality in case the child finds out about adult sex 'too soon', or because the parent is too embarrassed to answer questions, or because of the mistaken idea that this will keep them 'innocent' longer. Generation after generation of us has been controlled in this way – with the result that most of us are shy about sex. But many other aspects of a child can be controlled by this 'partial' ignoring – a child's need to be seen as beautiful, to look pretty or smart, to have the right kind of kit or uniform at school, to wear a bra because her friends at school have them, even though the parent thinks she isn't ready for one yet, to wear pretty panties instead of serviceable knickers.

The child's need to be popular can be ignored too – for example, its need to make friends and invite them home, to enjoy rough sports and get dirty, to be a tomboy, or the male equivalent of this. There are lots of children who spend most of their time out of harm's way playing at dolls and daydreams, dungeons and dragons, computers or construction kits in an upstairs bedroom. And there are many kids who grow up today knowing they will only get noticed if they perform – being very clever, clowning or telling jokes – everything else will be ignored. Inside they are very lonely. There have always been kids like this. Maybe you were one of them.

If you are the self-banishing type when you go into a depressive crisis, then the 'ignoring' method was used by your parents to discourage you. Again, the threat can be even more important than what the parent actually did to you. A child who is sent to its room may only be there for a short time, but if you were punished like this before you had any real idea of time, you would feel as though you had been sent away for ever – and your parent may have deliberately piled on the agony in order to make the punishment more effective. He or she may even have been laughing about it downstairs whilst your cries upstairs became more and more despairing. It happens.

Then there is the child who is threatened with being sent away for ever or never being spoken to again. If this was done to you, then you would have believed what was said, and felt all the lonely terror of the child who is truly unwanted. After all, the punishment would not have worked unless you thought it really would be carried out. If you ever feel today that you want to disappear for ever, to not exist and just fade away and never come back, if you 'just know' when your depression is at its worst that you are superfluous, that nobody really cares whether you live or die, the urge you feel began with these threats and punishments. What you wish to do to yourself now when you get depressed is what they threatened to do to you then.

There is no better guide to what was threatened than what you feel like doing to yourself at the worst moments of your depression – whether you succumb to the urge or not. If you feel like running away, if you 'switch off' and go numb and silent, then the threat was to send you away for good, or never to speak to you again. If you run away to the bathroom, a shed or garage, or your bedroom, then there was almost certainly a 'place of sin' to which you were banished each time you offended. You can probably remember exactly where it was. If your reaction is to feel uncomfortable and embarrassed in company, and to be afraid all the time of making a fool of yourself, then this is almost certainly because your parents used to become acutely embarrassed in case you 'showed them up in front of other people', or were disapproving whenever they thought you were 'showing off'. Maybe they said nothing – but would go tight-lipped and cold towards you, and pretend you were not with them. They probably never praised you when other adults were there unless they wished to take the credit for being good parents. Or, if they did praise you, they toned it down in case you became 'too big-headed', and if others praised you they devalued this. Or maybe they used to talk about you and criticize you in your presence, but as though you were not really there at all.

The self-rejecting reaction is sometimes delayed – you go to a party and enjoy it, but when you get home, you go over everything that happened and feel bad about it, even if you enjoyed yourself. If so, maybe you can recall the times your parents came home from an outing and held a detailed inquest, criticizing you, one another, or the people who were there, pulling them to pieces in respect of everything which had embarrassed them. Some depressed people in this group literally 'pull themselves to pieces' – when they are afraid they might have enjoyed themselves, they bite savagely at their fingers or pick at their skin leaving a raw patch which they then feel embarrassed about.

You may feel very awkward about your own body – that bits of it are too big or too small or very ugly. If so, these are the bits that were ignored by your parents in case you asked about them, or because these parts of you embarrassed them; or maybe they praised other people for looking good, but always ignored your own need to be praised or reassured about your body, particularly in adolescence.

If the 'ignoring' control method was regularly used on you, then an important part of your personality can be described as 'ignored'. Even when you are in the 'up' part of your cycle, you will still tend to use banishment as a defence against threats. Typically, ignored people are secretive. They have few really close friends, and see themselves as loners. In this way they banish themselves from the risk of being noticed too often. Many do not like to be touched – too much close attention makes them feel ill at ease, as if they are being 'pawed', or about to be punished. They are embarrassed by compliments – they cannot believe they have earned them and are afraid they are just being laughed at or set up for some kind of betrayal. Many feel safest when tucked away in some lost corner, in a place where they can work quietly and not be exposed to criticism, and many have become experts at things their parents would have found boring, or did not know enough about to be able to criticize confidently.

Some people, however, learned as children to avoid being ignored, and a major part of their personality has become the 'ignorer' type instead – the entertainers who 'make an entrance' where the rest of us would just go into a room, who turn their worst fears into jokes, and can tease an audience into laughing with them or at them, who always seem to be performing, off-stage as well as on-stage. They belong to the honourable ranks of the clown, fool, or jester – but only in public and when they are 'high'. Privately they are often depressed, and feel all the torments of the rejected and ignored child who is never taken seriously.

'RESCUE'

The third system of control is called 'rescuing', because it works by getting the child to rescue its parents from their own unhappiness. A good example is the parent who says to a child: 'Please don't do that, dear. You know I have a headache.' The child is made to feel responsible for causing the headache or making it worse, and it has to stop whatever it is doing in case this adds to the parent's pain. Another example is the mother or father who says, 'Please don't stop out late – you know it worries me.' As a result the child's choice of when to come home and how much to enjoy itself is restricted because it has to save its parent from worry. There are also many families in which the child is expected to make excuses for anybody who behaves badly: 'Your father didn't mean it, dear, it's just that he was tired,' or 'I'm sure the little boy who hit you didn't really want to hurt you,' and so on. All requests for favours have to be prefaced by the word 'please', and a receipt has to be issued afterwards with the words 'thank you'. Any sign of unhappiness on the part of somebody else has to be apologized for, with the word 'sorry', which the parent insists must be felt and not just said as an automatic or token response. Each time a rescue control is used the child has to put somebody else's needs first, and its own interests second.

In its mild forms, of course, you may think that this kind of control is no bad thing. Many families use it to teach children to grow up into considerate, well-mannered and responsible adults who are able to take account of the feelings of other people and who can see what effect their own actions may have on those around them. So at first sight this may not seem to be as cruel as 'squashing' or 'ignoring' a child. In its extreme forms, however, this method of control can turn childhood into a nightmare in which the child exhausts itself in the service of its parents, regards all the love it receives as conditional on its own good behaviour, becomes a little old man or little old woman under the weight of its responsibilities, and is willing to sacrifice everything, even its own life, to earn affection or relieve the pressure on others.

A child has no choice but to be dependent on its parents and to try to love them. At the heart of this system of control lies a cruel and dishonest exploitation of this need. A child can be deliberately made to feel responsible for every bit of unhappiness its parents experience. Each time it does something which displeases the parent it can be manipulated into feeling guilty because it has hurt them or disappointed them, so that it is constantly being taught that it does not deserve their love. Eventually the child believes this without question and grows up into an adult who feels unlovable, and always seeks reassurance that he or she is worthy of affection. To see how this is done, let us imagine a child who has 'behaved badly', and listen in whilst the parent, apparently more in sorrow than in anger, is trying to make it recognize its responsibility.

I can't understand how you could do such a thing. You are beyond belief! How could you be so selfish after all we've done for you? Just look at what you are doing to your poor mother! How do you think she feels? You are making her ill – you'll be the death of her if you go on like this. I don't know what the neighbours must think! Didn't you know that your mother is having a break-down just because of you – that you are driving your father into an early grave – your own father! We have made endless sacrifices for you because we love you. But what do you do in return? You just have to get your own way each time! Where you are concerned it's 'me, me, me!' You never seem to think about how other people might feel. They have needs, too, you know. You treat this place like a hotel – you can't even bother to tidy up your own room, and you know how your mother feels about that. There's no excuse for the way you behave – you must think we're just servants, paid to run around after you. We give you all our love, because we only want you to be happy, and all you give us in return is deliberate selfishness!

Dart after dart goes in like this – each one aimed at the child's need to give love and to be loved, and the tears which were held back at first begin to flow. The child sobs, but the parent goes on relentlessly, bitterly, until the sobs become an open sore of anguish and self-blame, the tears an unstoppable tide of guilt. Time after time, and in battle after battle, this is how the parent uses its child's need to give and receive love, pushing the child beyond tears into abject despair. In a series of lengthy power-struggles the guilt is worked on by the parent until it becomes such a permanent part of the child that a look of pain in the parent's eyes will reawaken the threat of yet another terrible, intolerable ordeal of accusation and moral blackmail.

The child is made to believe that it is responsible for the pain, the illness, even the death of those whom it fails to please, those to whom it was ungrateful, those for whom it was insufficiently sorry. The child brought up this way is crucified with sacrificial guilt. All it can do short of dying is cry and say it is sorry, or wear itself out in the knowledge that it will not and cannot ever be forgiven. It is never told that it has a right to be loved, a right to please itself and be irresponsible and foolish and self-seeking, a right to make mistakes – the right to be a child. It sacrifices its childhood because of its parents' inability to take responsibility for their own happiness.

Some children learn this lesson indirectly, too. They see what happens to their brothers or sisters or what one parent does to the other one, and they make up their minds to be 'good' so as to avoid this ever happening to them. They become people-pleasers who are terrified of letting their parents down after all they have done for them, or of disappointing anybody who needs them. Sometimes they are so 'good' that their parents hold them up as an example to their brothers and sisters – 'Why can't you be like Mary?'

The worst sin of all that a 'rescuer' child can commit is to be selfish, so the child is discouraged by being reduced to tears whenever it is caught pleasing itself or putting its own interests first. It lives by parental permission. Its main job in the family is to be the unpaid and willing servant, the good little girl or boy who helps mum or dad without complaining, or the child who holds the marriage together by carrying on the pretence that each parent is making the other happy, even when this is patently untrue. Every 'rescue' child is living proof for the rest of the world that its parents are good parents. It has to be 'good' to avoid causing its parents problems with anybody who might criticize them – the neighbours, for example, or their own parents, particularly if they live in the same house, or close enough for reports to get back to them.

In its most extreme versions the child willingly takes the blame for having caused all the problems its parents face, and feels guilty for the damage it has inflicted upon them by being born. At first it accepts full responsibility for their unhappiness, and tries to put matters right, so that the roles of child and parent are reversed, and the child looks after its parents and its brothers and sisters instead of the other way round. But when this proves to be insufficient, the child may kill itself to save the family from all the trouble it has caused. Nobody knows how many childhood suicides there are, but even one is too many.

If this kind of control was used on you, then even when you are coping with life, you will tend to be busily engaged in wearing yourself out with self-sacrificial duties. There is no time off for most rescuers – they are too busy doing good and trying not to expect gratitude. They are generous and concerned, supremely the 'people people' of the world – the ones who are sensitive and caring and polite, and who always find time to help others. They even help people who do not want to be helped. But the hardest and most courageous thing they can ever do is put themselves first.

If you cannot stop weeping when you go into a 'down', or if you ever find yourself desperate to please but miserable because you do not know how to, then you were trained as a rescuer – although, of course, it may not be the only way you were controlled. You had to earn love as a reward for service to others, so in a 'down' you feel unloved and unlovable. One large group of rescuers were conceived as 'reconciliation babies' by parents who were close to splitting up – having that baby meant they would have to stay together 'for the sake of the child', and ever after that, the child carries a heavy burden of responsibility wherever it goes in life. So if you get depressed because of all your responsibilities, you should suspect an early training as a rescuer. Also, if your job in the family was to keep your parents together, or to protect one parent from attacks by the other parent, then you too are a rescuer and you will be good at making excuses for people who behave badly. If you feel very anxious when people do not seem to like you, or always need permission to live your own life, then you were also brought up as a rescuer – almost all the things you wanted to do in childhood depended upon your parents' permission. To this day you cannot enjoy yourself without somebody else's permission in case you might become selfish.

DAMAGE

To sum up, the squashing control in childhood produces the self-violent reaction in the adult; the ignoring control leads to self-banishment; and the rescue control causes the self-sacrifice response. Of course, most of us had a mixture of controls – for example, it is quite common for a 'squashing' man to marry a 'rescuing' woman, so that their children grow up having to please mother by being good, and she leaves the beatings to father – the 'wait till your dad comes home' formula. Another common combination is the 'ignoring' mother who is busy outside the home enjoying her full-time career, or who dislikes – often for good reasons – having her life interrupted by motherhood, whilst a 'rescuing' father tries to manage the kids by asking them to be 'good' in order to help, and explaining how difficult things are for their mother. In many families one parent squashes the other. The father treats his wife rather like one of the children and she gets just as squashed as they do – many of us had a very strict or tyrannical father, and a mother who was 'beaten up' by him verbally or physically whenever she displeased him.

Obviously there are many more combinations, and you will have to work out for yourself what happened in your own family from your knowledge of your parents. Also, it is usually the case that one parent (or step-parent) – the dominant one in the matter of child-rearing – was more controlling than the other. So you also need to work out which one this was if you do not know already, since from this point on, when I refer to 'the parent' it will usually mean this dominant parent or parent-substitute.

But the main thing to remember is that what you do to yourself during a 'down' is the best guide there is to what happened to you in childhood. If you wrote down your main patterns at the end of the last chapter, now is the time to get out that bit of paper again and study it. You will have before you a list of the things which your parents used to threaten you with in order to control you. It is a basic principle in understanding people that as adults we do to ourselves and to others what our parents threatened to do to us when we were children. Some of these things are far more severe than others. The worst things you want to do to yourself are the result of discouragement from the parent who punished you most severely, and the less extreme things usually come from the other parent.

Whatever method or combination of methods your parents

used to control you, it is the threat of what might have been done to you which caused the damage rather than the actual punishment – although obviously they must have hurt you badly sometimes or this threat would not have worked. Some of this was done in the name of bringing you up the best way they could; some of it was the result of either or both parents losing control and blaming you. But you were taught to deny this, as they denied it, and will probably go on denying it if they are still around and you ask them for the truth. Do not deny it now – find out from the pattern of your own depression what their true legacy was to you, and decide if you wish to keep it.

And if you are reading this because you are the parent of a child who is depressed, then it is time you too accepted the truth about your own depression. Read the rest of this book for yourself, not to deny what you did, but to understand it. From now on your own parents should be your main focus; not your child. Until you recognize your own inner problems and start to tackle them you will, in any case, be unable to help anybody else who has similar problems, least of all your own children. I assure you that it's worth the effort: they will like you better when you have sorted yourself out. If you don't believe me, ask them.

The truth behind depression is, as I have said, shocking and disturbing. You might like to pause here, and let the truth touch you. You are not a helpless victim of these causes, because they can be undone, but you do need to understand them, not just in your head, but with your feelings too. Feel free. Feel free to be the person you and the rest of the world need you to be. You no longer have to spend your life wearing yourself out trying hard not to be the kind of person they did not want you to be, battering yourself, neglecting your own needs, giving away everything you get for yourself in order to help others who do not appreciate you. You are free to do what you want, to have what you need, to be who you really are. True – you are still in the cage, but now the door is open, and the bars are not what they seemed. Begin to feel free, and when you do, we can look together at that cage of yours and prise the bars apart.

Chapter Seven

WHO MAKES YOU FEEL DEPRESSED?

NOT WHAT BUT WHO!

You have almost certainly wondered many times, 'What makes me so depressed?' I hope you now accept that your ability to recover from the hard knocks of life was damaged during your childhood, so you react to loss and the threat of loss by feeling that you are useless, worthless, or to blame. During and since your childhood a chain of closely connected events has prevented this damage from healing, stopping you from learning how to recover from problems, and foiling all your attempts to be the kind of person you would really like to be. In your worst moments, you can see no way of changing this: you cannot stop being prone to depression, and you cannot see how to improve your circumstances.

But what about the triggers of depression? Can you do something about these? The answer is that you can, and you should. In childhood, what hurt you was the people who discouraged you, and this is still going on to this day. So the question you really need to ask now is not *what* makes you feel depressed, but who discourages you? Who is it that still uses parent-power to keep you under control? How did they get this power?

Now, of course, as with several of the questions we have looked at lately, I cannot answer this one in detail for you. Everybody who reads this will have a different set of people who trigger their 'downs'. You know far more about your own life than I ever shall. But what I can do is help you build up a list for yourself, and when you have it, I will show you what to do to stop those people inhibiting your recovery. So let's start on the list of people who threaten to squash you, ignore you, or make you rescue them. I'll make guesses, and you can see if I'm right.

PARENTS

Even when we are grown up, most of us still think of ourselves as belonging to the family we were born into. Not to be an active part of this family is still widely seen as something to be ashamed of. So if either or both of your parents is alive, there is a good chance that they still play an important part in your life. Perhaps you see them every day because you all live in the same house, or they live fairly close to you. Perhaps you telephone them, write to them, or visit them often. Maybe you and they get together less frequently, but make the effort to see one another every Christmas, or for family events. Millions of us keep in touch this way – and there are a great many of us who, if we are honest, have mixed feelings about doing so. All too often there is an element of 'reporting back' about such contacts, a kind of duty on our part to keep them informed of what we are doing so they can make judgements about us. We are supposed to respect their opinions about the way we run our lives – as if we were somehow living on their behalf. We have a responsibility to tell them all about the latest developments, and to show we are doing a good job. Failure on our part to keep them informed so they can judge what we are doing will be seen as evidence that we are rejecting them and do not wish to be 'family' any more.

Now, if any of this is true in your case, my guess is that whenever your parent or parents disapprove of something you have done, they still try to exercise control over you just as they did when you were little. There is a very good chance also that they succeed, if not every time then some of the time; that even though you are now grown-up, they can still make you feel small, using the same methods that they have always used. For example, if they *squashed* you as a child, then from time to time they will try to put you down the same way, with an angry word or gesture, or with a sharp command or a peremptory rebuke. If their main method of control was to *ignore* you, then when they want their own way, they probably still try to get it by going into a tight-lipped silence, or by making it clear that they will have nothing further to do with you if you argue. If they manipulated you into being a *rescuer*, then they can almost certainly still make you feel guilty just by looking or sounding hurt, by being ill, or by accusing you of being 'selfish', so you have to feel sorry for them and end up pleasing them rather than yourself. Whatever combination of all three they used, my guess is that they still use it.

The result is that every time the two of you get in touch with one another, you run the risk of ending up in crisis. Ask yourself when your last one began, and see if it could be connected with a talk you had with a parent. Of course, it might not be. But in fifteen years of working with depressed people as their therapist I have come to expect this, and nowadays I ask as a matter of routine. When my clients are distressed enough to phone me between sessions, a recent talk with a parent is nearly always the cause. The 'down' may start immediately, soon afterwards, or it might be delayed. For example, you might begin to feel frustrated, fed up, or furious while your parent is talking to you, and if you could only see or hear yourself, you would catch yourself sounding like a little girl or boy all over again, or producing all the defensive body language of a naughty child being rebuked. On the other hand, you might only feel this way after the parent has left, or, if it was a phone call, after you have put the phone down, becoming self-violent, going into a withdrawal, or feeling weepy and helpless once the conversation is over.

Or maybe you manage not to feel upset during or just after the talk, and bottle up your frustration. The problem with doing this is that it comes out afterwards in a different form. For example, you may find yourself later that day picking a row with your own kids, or fighting another losing battle with your spouse or spoiling for a quarrel with somebody at work who is bound to win. Or you might feel a strong urge to run away and never be seen again, or just to weep and ask yourself over and over what you have done wrong. Whatever your reaction is, if anybody asks you why you are in a bad mood you will probably say you don't know, so successfully have you suppressed recognition of the source of your anger. But no matter when the crisis takes place, if you have been subjected to an overdose of parent-power, sooner or later you start to become self-violent, self-banishing, or self-sacrificing as a direct result.

ABSENT PARENT

Of course, it could be that one or both of your parents is still alive, but you never see them. If so, then this is almost certainly because you dislike the way they try to control you. Families have always been more concerned with power than love, and people who have power are always reluctant to give it up – particularly parents, who may be starved of it except for the family. Many of us recognize this fact in our twenties, and put as much distance as we can between ourselves and our parents – maybe this is what you did. Nevertheless, you probably still feel that you ought to see more of them, or that you are wrong not to like them. Such thoughts can be very depressing, reminding you of what you lost because of the way they treated you.

Even if your parents are no longer alive, all this may still apply to you. When we grieve for parents, most of us have some reason to be angry with them, or at least to be disappointed at the lost opportunities for love which it is too late to put right. Dealing with this anger and disappointment – accepting it and being able to tell others about it so we do not have to bottle it up – is hard to do. Parents can anger and disappoint us long after we have left or they have died. So if your parents are still around, then they are almost certainly high on the list of the people who trigger off your 'downs'. On the other hand if they are not around any more, the need to deal with the anger you have good cause to feel towards them will help to make you depressed each time you are reminded of them.

It isn't just your parents. Other members of your original family can probably still affect your life the way they did when you were small – aunts and uncles, cousins, brothers and sisters who bossed you around, refused to have much to do with you, or who made you fetch and carry for them. You know your own family best, so you will have to ask yourself which parts of it still exist today, how this affects you, and whether any of these people should be on your list. It is not uncommon for early relationships to continue more or less unchanged into adult life, and for depressed people to feel threatened by events which show that their subordinate place in the family has not altered, in spite of everything they have achieved since. For example, you probably still feel bad when a more encouraged brother or sister does well and wins more approval than you ever received, or 'gets away with' something which you would not have been allowed to do or were brought up to regard as unthinkable. Or when one of your brothers or sisters is in trouble, and if it was your job as a child to look after him or her, you may still feel that it is your duty to drop everything and do a rescue act, however inconvenient or unfair this is on you.

THE DEPUTY PARENT

Members of your family are not the only people you need to put on your list; parents generally need help to bring up their children, to make sure they do the right things when the parents are not around. So they appoint deputies to act on their behalf, strangers who are empowered by them to control us 'for our own good'. We all grow up being told that certain people are set in authority over us – people whom we must respect, take notice of, or please: that is to say, accept as deputy *squasher*, deputy *ignorer*, deputy person to *rescue*.

One of the first deputy parents we meet is the teacher, and according to how we have been brought up, this is somebody we are told to obey, pay attention to, or help. Notice the squash, ignore, and rescue? Many of us have good cause to be grateful to teachers we have known – they are often the first people to encourage a depressed and unhappy child. There are also many people whose father or mother resented this and put an end to it, either by discouraging them from enjoying school, or by forcing them to leave too early.

But you may also have been discouraged at school instead of being helped, with school acting as just another extension of the controls imposed at home. Sadness caused by the gap between somebody's obvious intelligence and his or her lack of academic achievement is a common theme in depression. So if, despite your intelligence, you were unable to achieve very much at school, or if you hated exams and never went to college or university, and if you ended up educationally with second best or worse – then don't be surprised that anybody who acts in a school-teacherly fashion towards you or who patronizes you by talking down to you can trigger a crisis. Such reminders of what we have lost can make many of us feel self-violent, or self-banishing, or make us want to grovel at the time so we hate ourselves afterwards.

Or maybe you did well at school, but only if you ignored every other aspect of your life except scholastic achievement – and your teachers, just like your parents, ignored your need to be popular, to enjoy being an ordinary girl or boy. If so, you probably still feel lonely and defensive and embarrassed when the people around you seem comfortable with not being clever, when they easily produce small-talk, for example, or when they show what to you is an appalling ignorance of issues which matter. You may still have difficulty being ordinary, and a 'down' can be triggered every time you become aware of the gulf between you and most other people.

The teacher is only one example of a deputy parent – there are many more. Perhaps you can think of some of your own, and recall how you were taught to respond to them – and the pattern of squashing, ignoring, and rescuing that this entailed. For example, the doctor is one deputy parent many of us feel very strongly about. Squashing parents say we must do what the doctor tells us; ignoring parents that we should not feel embarrassed at being examined; rescue parents that we have to be careful to say how sorry we are to take up his or her time. As a result, the doctor is still somebody who can make us feel small, and contact with doctors and hospitals can lead to incidents which keep us angry and miserable for a very long time. Maybe you still feel hurt at being treated like a 'piece of meat', to be prodded and poked as if you were merely an object and not a person. Maybe you feel concerned about your physical health but ignore this rather than tell a doctor. Or maybe you have only good feelings about the medical profession, but still feel bitter and weepy at the time you came out of hospital after having a baby, or following an operation, and those whom you thought loved you just left you to cope.

We are also told that if we do something wicked, policemen will prosecute us; lock us up; make us regret what we have done. If we never break the law, then we are told that the police are there to crack down on criminals; to send them away for a very long time; to do a difficult job which we should be grateful for. Again, notice the squash, ignore, and rescue controls at work. As a result of these controls an encounter with the police is often a deeply humiliating experience, made worse by the way so many members of the force adopt the parent-power approach in their dealings with the public. Simply reading about a crime, or about crime statistics, can make some of us feel threatened far more than those who are not depressed would expect. Your own most recent crisis might have been triggered this way.

Because of this system of deputy parents, depressed people can often feel that they are surrounded by all sorts of hidden rules and regulations which they dare not break, and which entrap them. They constantly have to avoid behaviour which might turn them into the 'wrong' kinds of people, that is to say the kinds their parents would not have liked them to become. Quite often they do not realize that this is to do with parent-power, and see it instead as a matter of ethics or morality. Much of what they really want to do seems out of the question on moral grounds, when in fact it is only 'wrong' in the sense that it would have upset their parents all those years ago. Why does this happen? One reason is the way that religion is used in many families as an extension of parent-power. Religion and morality have been closely tied together throughout our history and, as we saw earlier, this link has long played an important part in the way parents bring up children. Religion and parent-power often team up together, as we can see from the fact that we still have many church schools, and in the way that an act of religious worship is by law the only compulsory item on the school curriculum in this country.

In the highest seat of Christian parent-power is God – a formidable trinity of control: God the Squasher, God the Ignorer, and God the Rescuer – the vengeful and creative Father of the Old Testament, who hurts us for our own good; the mysterious Holy Ghost, whose presence transforms, but whose absence punishes; and the sacrificial Son who died in redemption for our sins. Of course, this may not be what God is really about. But it is certainly the way many children are made to believe in God. So even when the parent who is mainly responsible for our control is absent, invisible forces take his or her place to control us for our own good using the same methods. God the invisible parent is the supreme authority. To break any rule is seen as wrong, and because God is all-seeing and all-knowing, we can never escape from being caught and punished. Can you remember believing this? Maybe you still do.

Of course, as we grow older, this awe of the deputy parent tends to fade, but it happens fastest amongst those who were encouraged to develop their own values: they begin to see quite early on that people in authority are only human after all. Many of us also begin to find our own ways of understanding God. We learn to appreciate love and to see that it is the very opposite of power and control.

But neither of these things is easy if we were seriously discouraged by our parents, so there are many depressed people who are intimidated very easily by any show of authority, and who have the greatest difficulty in breaking rules of any sort. If you are like this during a crisis, you will feel very anxious about doing or saying the wrong thing most of the time; or about making mistakes which will be noticed; or letting others down. Almost any display of power can make you feel you will never be able to win. For example, whenever you come up against officialdom in any form you will probably be unable to 'work the system'. You will generally have to tell the whole truth even if this costs you dearly. You will almost certainly not have learned to play petty officials at their own game – and you lose out all the time to rivals who are less scrupulous and feel able to make their own rules, or rebel confidently against other people's.

THE PSEUDO-PARENT

Parents and their deputies are not the only ones who have the power to control us. There is a third and more subtle extension of parent-power: the way in which we choose the people we share our lives with as a husband or wife, lover or companion. These people are not our parents – nor are they social authority figures. We appoint them ourselves. But the way we relate to them, and the way they respond to us, particularly in a crisis, none the less reflects the system of control which our parents used.

Our most important pseudo-parents are the people we marry. Nearly all first marriages are designed to continue the same type of control established by the parent. Power is handed over by our parents even to the people we think we have chosen just for ourselves, turning them into extensions of our parent's power. How is it done? They are quietly advised how to deal with us. The handover may take place when we get engaged, or just before the wedding, when the prospective father-in-law has a quiet chat with the husband-to-be, or the prospective mother-in-law briefs her son's girlfriend on how to treat him. Or it might take place when we hit our first marital crisis and our partners receive some kind of advice from our parents as to what to do. It may also occur when the children are born and we need parental help in some form or other, and our parent disapproves of some aspect of what we are doing. Sometimes the parent tells our husband or wife how they brought us up, and suggests that he or she should use the same methods on our children. If in doubt, and you can do so, ask your partner whether any of these happened.

But in any case, those of us who marry nearly always manage to choose somebody who uses on us the very same control pattern which our own parents used. There are several reasons for this. One is that our parents are most likely to approve of somebody as a prospective son- or daughter-in-law who has a similar set of values to their own, and very few of us are strong enough to marry somebody they do not approve of. Secondly, the parents of the person we choose also want somebody who will fit into their family – and we meet with their approval only if we seem to be the sort of person they can imagine as a son or daughter; that is to say, the sort of person who was brought up using similar controls to the ones they used on their own child, and who is still susceptible to these controls – somebody who was, in other words, 'properly brought up'. Thirdly, every marriage is an attempt to do the same kinds of things which were done in the original families of the husband and wife, although the couple often set out with the intention of doing them better. We can only achieve this if we use similar controls.

We may not be aware of all this at the time that we decide to get married or when we choose our partner – yet it even applies to those who marry against their parents' will. It all begins when we meet somebody and feel that he or she is a person we can get along with, someone with whom we have quite a lot in common, and where the 'chemistry' is right. But why do we feel this way? It is because we are already used to his or her pattern of control, the ways he or she deals with problems, the way such people run their lives, the prejudices they have, the values that they work from. The people we choose to become closest to seem in some way already familiar to us when we first meet them, so that we are much more likely to become friends or fall in love with them than with anybody else. It is only later, after we are living with them or married, that we begin to realize how easily they can exercise control over us by making us feel bad the way our parents did. Incidentally, if you have never married, and it isn't because you have not yet found somebody that your parents can accept, then it is probably because you feel uncomfortable with the whole idea of marriage, and the way it inevitably results in you being controlled.

Marriage is never easy, and the use of pseudo-parental controls – the way the dominant partner always tends to get his or her own way by behaving like the other partner's parent – is one of the main reasons for this. A great many of the crises that punctuate a depressed person's life are triggered by marital conflict. Disagreements with their partners often end up in self-violence, self-banishment, or self-sacrifice. The general rule appears to be that when we marry somebody, go to live with them, or form a sexual relationship with them, we apparently give them permission to take over from our parents as our main critics and controllers. Our real parents certainly seem to see things this way. So too do most parents-in-law.

There is another difficulty, too. We might be married to people we love, but do not *like*. If this seems a rather complicated idea at first sight, then consider the way a small child feels about its parents. It has to love them, but it may not actually like them, particularly if they are very controlling – extremely strict, very ignoring, or highly manipulative. Because marriages are so often repeat performances of childhood relationships with our parents, we can eventually feel the same way about our partners. Of course, most of us start off by loving and liking them, but the liking is much harder to maintain when they begin to control us. The more control there is, the harder it becomes to like them. Next, it gets harder to love them, and in time, love disappears too. We can end up staying together just because we are dependent on one another – the same way we had to stay with our parents when we stopped liking and loving them but could not leave home. But even if we find marriage under these circumstances intolerable, and get divorced, it can be years before we are freed from the ability of our ex-partners to control us by making us want to attack or neglect ourselves, or to rescue them. Husbands and wives, and ex-husbands and ex-wives are a very important element in the spider-web of parent-power, and the feeling of being trapped because of an unhappy marriage – even if it is over now – is a very commonly encountered trigger for depressive crisis.

There are other pseudo-parents in our lives. If you work at a paid job, consider your boss. The manager-subordinate relationship is a common example of pseudo-parenting. Any competent manager will soon find out which triggers to pull to control you – it's called 'motivating' you. As for the incompetent ones, they seem to do very little else but threaten people, not because they are good at motivating subordinates but because they enjoy the power that it gives them. It is easy to become trapped in an unhappy job, to spend hours of your 'free' time hurting yourself as you go over and over the latest ways you have been bullied or pressurized at work, or thinking of all the ways in which you are not appreciated.

Then there are the neighbours who know how to annoy you, make you wish you lived somewhere else, or whom you can spend all your time rescuing – or who manage to trigger your own particular combination of these controls. And all the strangers who want to get their own way by bullying us, acting as though we did not exist, or manipulating our need to be liked. You can meet them in shops, on the street, and particularly, if you drive a car, you will meet them on the roads. No doubt you can think of other examples of pseudo-parents who should be on your list. Each time they intimidate you, they remind you of the losing battles of your childhood, and make you wish to give in.

Chapter Eight

HOW CAN YOU CHANGE OTHER PEOPLE?

PEOPLE, NOT PROBLEMS

What can you do about these people? The answer is that you have to get them to change the way they treat you. Any one of them can trigger off another crisis, so that you write off all your recent gains – all he or she has to do is to threaten to squash, ignore, or manipulate you. So you have to stop them threatening you. There is no other way to begin if you are to make any lasting progress in your fight against depression. And I need to make this absolutely clear, since it is the most important point in the whole of this book. It is the way they treat you that you have to concentrate on first and foremost – not the way you respond to how they treat you. If a person threatens you, then what you must do is stop that threat – not find new ways of living with it so you feel less bad about it. You have to get them to change first.

The reason is quite straightforward. Only if you actually reduce the amount of threat coming at you, can you start to feel that you are winning. Trying not to feel bothered when people threaten you actually increases the risk. It acts as a challenge to them so they try even harder to get at you. This leaves you with no alternative but to try still harder not to feel intimidated. They raise the stakes too, and before you know it, you are spending all your time trying so hard not to feel anything that you might as well not exist. On the other hand, if you win sometimes instead of only fighting losing battles, this acts as such a boost to your morale that you begin to get the confidence to take charge of your whole life and change it.

The good feelings you gain each time you reduce somebody's

ability to threaten you are just what you want. You need to get lots of them, and to sustain yourself with them. I said at the beginning of this book that I would show you how to keep the gains you make in your periods of coping so that you can use them to deal with the crises. This is one of the things I had in mind. You need to use the best times to learn how to stop these people triggering off the worst times. What does this mean in practice? It means making sure that the next person who tries to gain an advantage over you by getting you to feel bad will fail in the attempt – or if not that one, then the one who tries it after that. And it means you have to do this whether that person is your spouse, your parent, or a stranger, and whether he or she does it deliberately or not.

FOUR METHODS

There are, in general, four ways of dealing with people who try to control you. First, you can *avoid* that person, stay out of his or her way altogether, and if this is just not practical, have as little as possible to do with the person. Secondly, you can *confront* whoever is trying to control you. This means standing up to the person and being more aggressive. Thirdly, you can attempt to *trade*, that is to say, to go for a 'give-and-take' solution, by negotiating with the person to reduce the threat. The fourth method is to *empathize* – to get to know the other person better, and help him or her get to know you better at the same time, so you both learn to trust one another more. Incidentally, the easy way to remember the four is by using the initial letter of each – ACTE. By a happy coincidence this is a French word that means 'Do it!'

What I am suggesting is that whenever somebody makes you feel bad, and whoever that person is – a parent, a husband or wife, a brother or sister, a neighbour or a stranger – you should choose the method which will be the most appropriate under the circumstances, and use it. We can look at how to choose the right method later, but before we do so, there is another point that has to be made. You should begin here and now by being willing to use any of the four methods. The wrong way is to put yourself at a disadvantage by ruling out any single method for the rest of your life either because it has not worked for you so far in that relationship, or because you do not have the skill, or because it simply isn't you. This reaction is understandable, but it will tie one hand behind your back.

Never to use *avoidance*, for example, would be to cut out from your repertoire the best way you have of controlling the number of threats in your life. But some people object to it because it seems to be too passive a response, others because they say that is what they always do and it is time they stopped running away, and some because they would feel very guilty avoiding people who need them. Also, you might not like the idea of *confronting*, maybe because you are afraid of getting too aggressive and ending up hurting somebody, or because you have been hurt in the past whenever you have tried it. Some people react just as badly to the idea of *trading*, because whenever they attempt it, they always seem to end up with the worst deal. Others feel uncomfortable with the idea of *empathizing* because it depends on them becoming more vulnerable, or because it can seem manipulative and unprincipled.

Why is it that people feel bad about particular methods? The answer is that it is connected with the main form of control used on them as children. For example, people who are very bad at confronting tend to be those who were badly squashed in childhood. They know they will need all their courage to stand up to somebody who is bullying them, because they learned very early on that their role in life was to be the bullied person, not the bully. In their case learning to confront will be a brand new skill, but this does not mean to say they will be unable to learn it, just that it might take them longer to do so. Similarly, if you feel bad about the idea of trading with the person who threatens you, then this will almost certainly be because you will have to reveal the fact that you feel threatened. This isn't easy for any of us, but it is especially hard if you were brought up with mainly 'ignore' controls, since your strongest impulse when threatened is to self-banish, and hide your feelings. You might have a similar attitude towards using the empathy method for much the same reasons.

Without going into all the ins and outs of this, the fact is that you need to learn a new expertise in all four of the skills, regardless of the methods your parents used on you. However, you should be aware of the fact that at least one of the four will be particularly difficult for you, and therefore you will need more encouragement to use it. In the meantime, try not to be put off – remember that your objective is to be equally good at all four. It will help if we look in more detail at each of the methods.

AVOIDANCE

In theory, if you can cut out from your life all the people who threaten you, you will cease to be threatened. But in practice, most of us who get seriously depressed would have to cut out everybody, since everybody is a potential threat to us. This would mean not only severing our links with all the people we know already, but also refusing to have any contact with strangers. We would end up totally isolated, and that would do us no good at all, even though it might appeal to the 'ignore' types amongst us.

So think of avoidance as a skill. The challenge is to find clever ways of having less contact with people who have the power to hurt you – withdrawing from them, and becoming more independent of them. You need to do three things: to reduce the energy which you spend on such people; to put a greater distance between you and them, either physically or emotionally or both; and to spend less time with and on them. To be able to do all three is best, but you will be doing well if you manage two of them, and accomplishing only one of them is still worthwhile.

There are several ways of reducing the amount of energy you spend on people. For example, it is a good idea to stop working so hard to explain yourself to people when they seem to be criticizing you, to cut back on any activities which you feel you have to do for them but dislike doing, and to redirect rather more energy into pleasing yourself. If you cannot avoid somebody completely, then just do less with them and for them. Put less energy into talking to them, listening to them, and maintaining contact.

Increasing the distance between yourself and people who threaten you can be done by physical means – keeping out of their way more often, not going to places where they will be most likely to see you, sitting or standing further away when you talk, and so on. The way to increase emotional distance is by showing less interest in them and their activities, even if this seems impolite, and they accuse you of being stand-offish. The plus side is that it should enable you to make more space for yourself, and to use it in ways which give you pleasure. Spending less time with somebody means just that, but there are many ways you can do it. For example, tell white lies to get phone calls or meetings cut short, or say you have done something they wanted you to do, even if you haven't done it, just to shut them up. If you haven't any good reason for leaving when you want to go, make one up – however unlikely – give it, and leave. Am I encouraging you to lie? Yes, I am!

And for good reasons, too. As I said earlier, depressed people are bad at breaking rules which non-depressed people break continuously. They tend to be particularly over-sensitive to minor moral issues. So if this applies to you, it is time to learn to break the rules. Don't be afraid of it becoming too much of a habit. A few white lies will not turn you into a pathological liar in spite of what your parents told you when you were having your character built. What is more, there is no all-seeing, all-knowing, invisible presence which will make a note of your small sins in a large book and make sure you get punished. If there is such a presence, then it loves you and wants you to feel better – and that means it won't let on to the people you lie to, either.

You also need to learn how to cut down on promises to do things to help people. Do what you can for them while they are there, but don't promise to work hard for them while they are enjoying themselves. You will resent this, and they will take you for granted, which is bad for both of you. Remember also that spending less time on other people is only worth doing if all the time you save is spent pleasing yourself, even though you will probably feel guilty about this, and afraid it might become a bad habit – and you ought to know by now where this feeling comes from. So right now, who can you cut out of your life, and to what extent? Think about the people who threaten you, and make up your mind.

CONFRONTATION

Confronting means literally standing up to somebody, brow to brow. In practice it means showing somebody who makes you feel threatened that you are angry about what he or she is doing. To confront somebody you have to be aggressive or assertive. Aggression and assertiveness are different ways of showing anger. The best way to learn about being more assertive is to attend an assertiveness workshop. You can also study the books mentioned in the reading list. Many people are afraid of confrontation because they are scared or ashamed of their own anger, even when they have every reason to feel angry.

The key point about aggression is that it is better to show it openly than to bottle it up and risk it coming out later and hurting the wrong target. There are several ways you can do this. The mildest of all is to tell the person who makes you feel threatened that you are feeling angry, and would like to explain why. You try to do this in a very calm, relaxed voice, and gently insist on being heard. Or at least, some people try to – and the chances are that nobody takes any notice. The way to tell somebody that you are angry is to sound angry, and to look angry, and the angrier you feel, the more angry you should sound and look. On balance, however, it is best to say you feel angry as soon as you start to do so, and not to wait until you get so cross that you have to scream and start throwing things. One of the best signs that you are starting to be angry with somebody is when you begin to have to make an effort to be patient. That is almost always the right time to say something about how you feel.

The whole purpose of aggression is to hurt somebody exactly as much as that person has hurt you – no less and no more than this. Getting it right isn't easy at first – it takes a lot of skill. You might fall short of the target, or go over the top. If either of these two things happens your adversary will not know precisely how angry you feel, and neither of you will be able to make the right kinds of judgements about what to do next. So if you fail to use enough aggression, you have to get angrier and angrier until that person has been hurt by you exactly as much as he or she hurt you. If you go over the top what you have to do is correct the balance by saying that you did not mean to be quite as hurtful as that, but you still insist on him or her knowing exactly how much you were hurt. But remember: never apologize for showing the right level of anger, only for the bit that exceeds this level. And don't be put off by the knowledge that the other person did not mean to threaten you. The fact is, he or she did threaten you, and only if that person fully understands this will there be a chance of it not happening next time. Of course, this is unfair sometimes, and you will have to make amends. But do this later, after you have confronted the person, rather than before.

It might help to summarize briefly how to show anger, since there are many depressed people who have never really known how to do this. What you do is not to hit people with your fists, or kick them – indeed, you will be safer if you can avoid physical contact altogether, so stand far enough away to make sure that neither of you can land a blow. The best way is to hit out with your eyes, and with your voice. Poke your opponent with your eyes. I call it 'eye-zapping': you use your eyes like a ray-gun. At the same time, punch out the message as if each word was a fist. Let your face do whatever it needs to do to allow your eyes to zap and your voice to punch. Also, let your body look as though you would attack if you were close enough. If you want to swing your arms about, bend forward, or clench your fists, then do so. Say how you feel, and what you want done about it. Keep your sentences short, swear if it helps, make your point, and as soon as it is made try to calm down.

To do any of this you may need to give yourself permission to look undignified. Nobody who really shows the anger he or she feels can stay dignified – those who appear to do so are lying. You won't sound reasonable, either. Anger is always unreasonable – that's the whole point of it. So let yourself be unreasonable and irrational.

A lot of people worry about losing self-control. But it is no bad thing to do this now and then – you'll get it back. You won't go off the rails permanently. The fear you feel is because you have probably never lost control since the great power struggles of child-hood, and all it means is that you are out of practice. You will soon learn how to lose control and how to get it back – your body remembers, even if your mind doesn't. Don't forget that the in-ability to lose control can keep you depressed by stopping you from attempting confrontation. As a result, even those people who care about you, and who would be very concerned and want to help, may simply not know that you get angry with them – or, at least, have no idea how often or how much. Surely it is kinder and more honest to let them find out, even if you risk blowing a fuse. Fuses are easily mended, anyway; that's what they're for.

One thing is certain – if it is a very long time since you showed aggression towards anybody, you are not going to be perfect at it the first time you do it. Confrontation is a skill, and like all skills, it gets better with practice. You will be very lucky to hit the target perfectly the very first time you try it, and most people go through a period of underestimating and then overestimating the amount of aggression they have to show to make their point. You can expect this; it need not prevent you trying. The best way to start anything new is to begin by doing it badly. If you try to begin by getting it right straight away then you won't begin at all. Who can *you* start with?

TRADING

The purpose of trading is to come to an agreement or 'contract' with a person who makes you feel threatened that both of you can accept, and that both of you will try to stick to in future. You do this by offering to do something which will benefit the other person in return for something of equal value to you. For example, you might tell your husband that if he stops raising his voice when telling you to do something, you will work harder at not forgetting what it is he wanted from you. Or you might propose that you will do more favours for your mother, and do them more efficiently in future if she asks you straight – without her making out that it is a special favour for which she will be eternally grateful, or that she is only asking because she is near death's door and would not trouble you otherwise.

The most important point to remember about trading is: plan ahead. Contracts thought up on the spur of the moment are less likely to succeed. They are more likely to come over as sarcasm or some form of protest than as genuine offers, and this will put you at a disadvantage. So you need to have a good idea of the various steps which are involved before you start, and to have thought things through thoroughly.

Firstly, you have to work out in advance, and for yourself (perhaps with independent help), who it is that you want to make a contract with. That is to say, think of somebody who makes you feel bad, think about what he or she does to trigger this feeling – usually, an irritating habit, such as a gesture or turn of phrase – and decide how you would feel if this trigger were never used on you again. Go for something specific – not the person's attitude in general but something he or she does which actually shows.

Secondly, you need to work out what advantage you can offer the other person. What is it about you that annoys him or her? You will offer to do your best to avoid this in future. Whatever it is, however, it should be directly connected with the trigger – something you do as a response to the threat itself. For example, if a spouse makes you feel bad by talking about you as if you were not there, and you usually respond by not being around when you know you can help, you could offer the advantage of being there to help more often, in exchange for being ignored less often. But don't offer something unconnected. If being talked about in this way does not make you criticize that person's mother – even if you are her worst critic – then do not offer to stop doing this in exchange. Also, avoid making vague, general offers – that you will love the person more, for example, or be kinder in future. You should only offer things you can do and be seen to do – the sort of things you can actually count when you do them. That way you will be able to keep a record if necessary and prove that you have stuck to your part of the bargain. It is worth adding also that certain kinds of offer are best kept out of such contracts – such as unswerving and uncritical support for all time, the suppression of any of your own feelings, and access to sex. Keep these for free gifts.

The third step is to make the offer. Choose a moment when the other person seems to be in a reasonable frame of mind and say you want to make a suggestion. Then make your offer. It is a very important principle of all negotiation that if the other person says no, the deal is not made, and there are no hard feelings on either side. So you have to be prepared to explain fully, and only to take no for an answer once you have spelled out your offer, but then to do so without feeling irritated. Don't let failure to make one deal put you off suggesting other contracts in future. And remember that even if you fail to make a deal, you will probably benefit, since the other person may have no idea that the behaviours you want to negotiate about are in any way connected – that the way you irritate him or her is a direct result of what is so often done to you. You might even get what you want without having to trade. By the way – leave all the clever stuff like offering less at first and increasing your offer later to the experts.

The fourth step is about keeping to the contract. Do your best to deliver your side of the bargain, but if the other person fails to, then the deal is off. You need to say so as soon as this happens, and not make a great issue of it. Never let it go on with you saying nothing while the anger or frustration builds up inside you. Of course, this might be what you do at first, simply because you are learning and cannot expect to do everything right straight away. So if you find yourself getting angry, break off the deal, and tell the other person you have done so, but without showing this anger. Fifthly, try to find out through reasonable discussion why it went wrong. Then, if possible, set up a contract that is easier to keep. Who is it, right now, that you could usefully trade with?

EMPATHY

The paradox of human conflict is that we can often reduce our vulnerability by becoming more vulnerable. This is because we like people whom we know can hurt us, but who never do. We trust them. Equally, people tend to like us if we can hurt them, and yet be trusted not to do so. The 'empathy' method means getting to know people better in order to build mutual trust.

How do you go about this? In theory the last people we feel able to get to know better are those who make us feel threatened, but in practice it is often quite easy. First, you have to admit to the person that you feel threatened by him or her. This might come as a complete surprise to that person, so that there is not much else you need to do – he or she may have been quite unaware of how you felt, and will try to put things right in future. Or the other person may be relieved because, although you did not know it, you were also a threat to him or her, and once this has been said the tension is reduced on both sides. But if none of this happens, the second step is to say that you like the person enough to want a better relationship, and again, provided you explain what kind of change you want – for example, to be more polite, to respect one another's property more, to be treated less like a child – this may be enough. Just spelling out your feelings will improve the relationship by making each of you more receptive to the other. If neither of these two moves does the trick, then, thirdly, you have to say clearly that a better relationship can only come about if you make a determined effort to get to know one another better. Of course, none of this will work at all unless what you say is sincerely meant, and it won't work unless the other person also wants it to work. The surprising thing is how many of the people who threaten you also feel threatened *by* you but haven't said so. They are pleased when you take the initiative.

It is not easy for people in a close relationship to start to make important changes in their lives. To build or rebuild trust you need a time and place where you both feel safe enough to talk frankly. For example, it often helps to be alone with the person, preferably on safe neutral ground. Make as sure as you can that you will not be interrupted for at least an hour. Small details can be very important; it is best, for example, that you both use similar chairs so that one of you is not in any sense looking down on the other. Once you start, it is important to get the other person to talk by being prepared to open up about yourself, and by listening well. Try not to ask long and complicated questions – just use short prompts, such as 'I would like to hear more about that', and 'How did that make you feel?' And try not to be afraid of long silences. Don't rush in and fill them each time they happen. The people we trust are those with whom we can be silent; long, thoughtful pauses are a sign of progress.

Whatever you do, try to understand the other person without making moral judgements, and make it clear that anything that you are told will go no further. Try to get him or her to talk from the heart and, when it is your turn, reveal a similar amount about yourself. It is particularly useful to get the other person to talk about childhood, and for the two of you to swap experiences of that time in your life. You will almost certainly find that you both have a lot more in common than you realized.

Empathy really means 'one-feeling' – the feeling that you are both 'at one' with the world, and this is what you both need to aim for while you talk. But even if you achieve this, particularly with somebody you have not been close to before, remember that it does not have to lead to a lasting friendship for it to be worthwhile. Make this clear, and agree that both of you can be content with the here-and-now feeling of not being threatened by one another during the conversation – and try not to pin too much hope on this lasting afterwards. You will still have defused many of the threatened feelings you started with, and dealing with threats from that person will be easier afterwards because you will have a truer idea of where they come from. It is important to say this too: all such sessions should be kept sexually neutral, even with a lover or spouse. Concentrate only on increasing trust, and during the session, take care to avoid any action which might be taken for a sexual come-on. So who is it right now that you need to get to know better in order to increase mutual trust?

NEXT STEP

To sum up so far, the A C T E approach gives you a choice of four methods of reducing the threat from people. But there is still a long way to go before you can use it effectively, particularly when you try it out on people who think they know you very well. Also, each technique has its own risks, which you need to know about. So the next step will be to help you decide how to choose the most appropriate method, depending on how you are being threatened.

Chapter Nine

HOW CAN YOU IMPROVE
YOUR CHANCES?

SPECIALISTS

Most of the people on your list are probably 'specialists' – they specialize in using only one type of threat, either squashing, ignoring, or getting you to rescue them. Some will use two out of the three, but only a small proportion are equally good at all of them. What I am going to do next is show you how to recognize the specialists, and then discuss the best ways of tackling them – whether it helps to avoid them, and where it is better to confront, trade, or empathize with them. In describing the specialists, I shall present caricatures and stereotypes rather than scientific observations – this is to help you learn quickly how to recognize each type for yourself.

RECOGNIZING SQUASHERS

Those people who specialize in using squashing controls on others are called squashers. How can you recognize them? Each squasher grew up in a family where the main system of control was physical punishment or the verbal threat of physical punishment. He or she was taught to respect the parent, and to obey instructions. But instead of being discouraged all the time, most squashers received enough encouragement to grow up into successful people.

From the outside they appear confident, self-assured, and able to bounce back in adversity. They are energetic, hard-working, and want practical answers to each problem. They see themselves as natural leaders who enjoy responsibility. They show intolerance of theorists, dreamers, and do-gooders. To a squasher there is always a right way of doing everything, and this is the way he or she would do it. They always tell you to do it this way, too – they like telling other people what to do. They cannot bear to see people being idle – it gets to them, and converts them instantly into bullying pseudo-parents.

'Doing' – as opposed to 'having' or 'being' – is the most important thing in a squasher's life. So, if you want to motivate a squasher, give him or her more to do; to upset one, take responsibilities away, or prevent them from being exercised. They are not interested in having something for its own sake, and tend not to notice objects which are merely decorative. Nor are they much attracted to 'being' for its own sake – they are so bad at just 'being there' that they cannot sit still even when they are supposed to be resting. They hate being ill, and get impatient when other people are ill. Their response to depression is to try to bully you into being more cheerful – they order you to look happy. Do you recognize anybody?

Squashers seldom know their own strength. Sexually they are energetic and purposeful, but their own purposes usually come first, and they cease abruptly to be energetic once these have been fulfilled. Around the house they are workmanlike do-it-yourself types. They drive aggressively and swear at other road-users. They like noisy, busy jobs, with lots of other people around, and which offer physical challenge or danger, and give them authority – you will find many of them in the armed forces or the police. Those who were disciplined as children with a hard slap and no fuss turn into the bluff, honest, straightforward type; those who were 'indirectly' squashed are devious. They all have to win, even at Snap with the kids. The indirect squashers cheat. Are you married to somebody like this?

A squasher's first response when faced by a problem is to demand to know who caused it. But once they have calmed down they can often be persuaded to think it might have been their fault. In fact they are often willing to listen to criticism, but it has to be timed right, constructive, practical, and directly relevant to a problem they want to solve. They claim to know themselves very well, but add that they are always ready to learn something new. Life for many of them has always been a tough school, and they are proud of their hard-won common sense.

We all give out signals constantly on many different wave-lengths – signals about what we are going to do next and how we shall do it, about what we have and how we are going to get what we want, about who we are and how we feel – the 'doing', 'having', and 'being' of our lives. These signals add up to 'body language'. How can you read body language to spot a squasher? Because squashers are mainly do-ers, their body language is all 'crash, bang, wallop' – full of impact, creating a series of short, sharp shocks. They seem to do everything with a punching, hard-hitting, slapping, poking, prodding, kicking, chopping, elbowing kind of style. This is how they talk, and it is also how they gesture, how they look at people, shake hands, sit down or stand up, walk, shift objects out of their way, and deal generally with other people. Everything about them is forthright, no-nonsense, clear the decks for action, wham bang thank-you ma'am.

DEALING WITH SQUASHERS

Do you recognize anybody on your list, and if so, what are the best ways of dealing with him or her? Avoiding a squasher is easiest if you are prepared to be written off by him or her as useless. The price you have to pay is that once the squasher has washed his hands of you, nothing about you will be respected by him or her ever again, and there may be a short period in which you are treated with great scorn or some physical violence. Once this part is over, squashers generally go off and find something else to do, but in the meantime their tantrums look dangerous. The amount of physical violence you can expect at this stage varies greatly – some of them just make threats. But you may be un-fortunate enough to live with an extreme example of the type – somebody who regularly beats you up, hits the children, turns your home into a concentration camp, and makes you afraid for your life. If this is happening, what should you do about it?

First, it has to be said that living with an extremely violent and threatening squasher is never worth it: one day one of those tantrums could kill you, literally. So if you already know this in your heart, get some help; tell somebody, preferably somebody with experience of wife or child battering, take what you can carry in a plastic bag, and get out. I know it's difficult, particularly if you are a rescuer, but try to realize that it was not your fault the relationship failed. If somebody hits you it is his or her fault, even if you think you may have provoked it. There are many other ways of responding which the person could have used; he or she did not have to use physical violence, but chose to do so.

But with relatively mild squashers, you may not want to leave. Can avoidance still help you? The answer is that where squashers are concerned piecemeal avoidance often causes more problems than it solves. They are often too thick-skinned to notice when you cut down the amount of energy, space, or time you share with them unless you do this drastically, and if they do notice, then being written off by them and being treated with contempt may make matters worse for you. In my experience, the most effective way of stopping a squasher from threatening you is to confront – to stand up to the person and hurt back. Getting the right amount of hurt is very difficult at first, particularly if the person thinks he or she knows you very well, so make sure that you correct immediately for any short-fall. But don't worry about overdoing it. Squashers do not know their own strength, and often underestimate other people's. It's no bad thing for them to think you are stronger than you really are.

But don't stop at confronting. Catch them by surprise, hit hard, and then immediately change your tactics while the surprise lasts, by appealing to their willingness to accept constructive criticism and practical solutions to real problems. For example, if a squasher is making those typical poking or prodding gestures at you, or raising his voice and shouting when telling you to do something, lift up your hand like a traffic policeman and say in a loud voice, 'Stop!' Hit out with your eyes, and keep your face looking stern. Repeat this until you get a look of surprise. Then say that you are not going to be talked to like this because it will get both of you nowhere. Add that you have always thought of him or her as a practical, common-sense, down-to-earth person, but that talking to you like this always stops you listening. You will probably be asked how you want to be talked to – in which case say without sarcasm that you are pleased to be asked, and explain. If he (or she) says he will talk to you any way he likes, let him start again, and then say 'Stop!' once more. Refuse to do anything until you have been listened to, even if he or she shouts or bangs the table. When exasperation sets in at last, seize your chance and act as the other person's exact equal, regardless of any actual status difference, and either suggest a deal, or suspend proceedings until you know one another better.

Of course, this is only one example. You will have to use your own ingenuity to invent similar tactics which work for you with the particular squasher you have in mind. The main principle is: squash back, get the look of surprise, and follow up either by making a give-and-take contract or 'trade', or by proposing a get-to-know-you-better session immediately or later. It is important to get your timing right, and to attack with surprise on your side, so it will pay you at first to go for those moments when the squasher is unaware of coming across as angry or bullying, and to avoid moments when he or she is very upset. Try picking up those casual orders which squashers issue without thinking – 'Listen!' instead of 'I would like to say something,' or 'Come here!' instead of 'May I talk to you?'

Counter-squashing the squashers can be daunting at first. With practice, however, you will learn how to do it even when your squasher is bellowing like a mad bull. The fear will grow less in time, although at first you will probably have to suppress it. Don't forget that the overwhelming majority of squashers have a bark that is worse than their bite, and that this one in front of you is not in charge of your life and cannot really hurt you as long as you stand up to them. One very old method of reducing fear works well with squashers – imagine them dressed in underpants, or sitting on the loo, or as babies, not as monsters!

The trading and empathy methods are ultimately your best bet, but even with mild squashers, you will generally find that 'biffing' them first, however gently, will improve your chances. And there is a special kind of delight in store for you the first time you manage to confront a squasher, catch him or her on the hop, and see that mouth drop open in total surprise! You might as well enjoy this – it is the first step in a new relationship with somebody who will probably become a more generous friend in the future, and who, within reason, will do anything for you. Squashers are loyal and supportive allies once they respect you, but they need regular booster doses of 'biffing' to keep them in line.

RECOGNIZING 'IGNORE' TYPES

A child may be controlled by ignoring, by deliberately not talking to it, by not acknowledging it as a person, by not recognizing certain of its needs, by wilfully forgetting or by withholding promised rewards. People who threaten you by using these controls divide roughly into 'ignorers' who are extroverts, and 'ignored' who are introverts. Both grew up in families where they were sufficiently encouraged to be clever at using the same controls on other people.

Ignore types prefer 'having' things to either 'doing' or 'being' – they are nearly always collectors – ignorers collect money, gadgets, and consumer durables, and the ignoreds collect secrets, skills, or curios. To motivate either type, pay them more; to demotivate, pay them less or overcrowd them. They both like big houses, large offices with huge desks, big gardens, lots of space around them all the time. The ignorers keep the space empty to create vistas, while the ignoreds fill it untidily with objects. Does this help you recognize anybody on your list?

Some ignorers are natural comedians, salesmen, or gamblers and can be found in any bar telling jokes – not stories about themselves, but jokes – surrounded by cronies, and resisting any relationship that is not superficial. They also like practical jokes with a streak of cruelty just below the surface. They may not admit it, but they don't really like people – deep down they mistrust most of them. Their world is often divided into two parts – a very small circle of close friends, and the 'punters' – the fools born every minute who can be taken for a ride. The quieter ignorers are charmers – suave, urbane, and cultivated, like all those doctors, lawyers, dons, or politicians who appear on television wearing a bow tie or a silk scarf. They love to issue pronouncements where you have to work out what they mean while they smile enigmatically. This is very threatening if you are dependent on them for information. They are often miserly even if all you need from them is a word of thanks or a cuddle. They give away very little and have clever and suspicious minds. Picture them as spies or diplomats. As sex partners, ignorers perform well but play you like a violin, or are efficiently clinical.

The ignored ones are skilled craftsmen who carry some mark of their trade with them and seem to hide behind it – the folding ruler falling from a pocket, the large bunch of important-looking keys, or the paint-stained overall, for example – or shy experts at something very difficult to do, such as computer programmers, accountants, actuaries, librarians, archivists, or inventors. They are renowned for getting on with a job quietly and with total concentration and great attention to detail. A lot of them find sex too trivial, too messy, or too threatening for them to be very interested, so they seem bored by the whole thing. But some are shy at first, then secretly passionate – they like to do naughty things under the sheets. Recognize anybody?

Ignore types have characteristic body language too. The ignorers are 'laid back', and sit like a puppet whose strings are broken, or uncoil themselves slowly, like one of those speeded-up films of a plant growing. When angry, they tend to use a lot of pressure in their voices and in the way they gesture or look at you – pushing you, pulling you, looking past you instead of at you, or simply cutting you dead. The ignoreds are often so quiet you wonder if they ever use body language. When angry they freeze up even more, and seem immovable. Who do you know like this?

DEALING WITH IGNORER AND IGNORED TYPES

Avoidance is easy – but that isn't usually the problem, because they are better at it than you, and the chances are this is what threatens you about them. For example, the 'expert' who avoids telling you things, the boss who jokes his way out of tight corners and disappears, and the parent who refuses to have anything to do with you unless you give way – each of these is a threat because you cannot pin him or her down. But if you want to use avoidance, when your adversary threatens to disappear for good let him or her go, cut your losses, and breathe a sigh of relief. It may well be the last you see of the person – unless there is a climb-down on his or her part, and that will be a victory for you to accept gracefully.

Confrontation can work well, but there are two problems. The first is that ignore types are easily shocked by any display of raw feelings, and seldom admit this. So if you get angry the other person will probably look very puzzled, and you will think you have gone too far. Don't be misled – the look of bewilderment usually means you have hit your target, and given time to find a good excuse for themselves they will climb down. The second problem is that this type includes some of the world's best logicians – the people who turn every argument into a debate, and who 'win' by using superior reasoning power, and by underestimating the importance of feelings. So if, after looking puzzled, they tell you coldly to calm down, and then use logic to prove that they are right and your own anger is misplaced, just stick to your feelings and insist that your anger is real, and they have caused it, and ask them to stop causing it. When logic fails, they turn remote and sarcastic, or just dig in their heels, and say they are fully entitled to do what they want whether this upsets you or not. Answer this by saying that you are just as entitled to your anger, and you will go on showing it every time you feel they have caused it. Don't give in – they can be very stubborn, and you have to be more stubborn.

Because they are often unhappy when faced with emotion, the ignore types are hard to confront without a lot of practice on your part. The best way to stop them threatening you is to trade, that is to say, to do a deal with them. This appeals to their sense of being logical, reasonable people, and provided that you are willing to haggle and, at times, to let them feel they have the best of the bargain, they will agree deals which you can benefit from. For example, both ignored types have the habit of 'dropping you' – acting as though you did not exist – as soon as they have said what they want to say. This can seem very impolite. It also means that if you wait your turn, they are off before you get your chance to speak, and you are left open-mouthed whilst they go away uninformed. If you explain this to them, and suggest that when you have something to say to one another you should always start, they will often agree and try to stick to the arrangement.

Ignorers tend to cover up feelings by joking, or get you to forget your own feelings by making you laugh. Tell them that in future you would like to separate business from pleasure – that if you are to understand how they feel, you need to be told honestly. Suggest that talking about feelings should come first and jokes second. Promise to laugh at the jokes only if they stick to this arrangement. Don't be misled by humourless laughter – it always means that the person is feeling threatened.

I shall have to leave it to your own ingenuity to devise other 'trades'. There isn't space for more examples – and in any case, you can be sure they will read the book too, and enjoy thinking of clever contracts for themselves. So always try to use time spent with this type on increasing empathy. The rules to remember are these. First, don't get side-tracked into listening to long, funny stories, detailed rationalizations, or complicated analogies: don't let the other person 'head-trip'. Second, insist on knowing about the other person's feelings: 'I think' is unacceptable; 'I feel' is what you want to hear. Third, acknowledge the other person's cleverness and courage, and give all the honest compliments you can, but don't expect him or her to show pleasure at this. It will be felt, but not revealed. Fourth, don't try to get close too soon. Stay back physically, but smile and show a lot of warmth in your voice and your eyes. With very tall ignore types, always talk sitting down. Fifth, look out for shyness – ignoreds are often shy, or used to be once. It shows in underdeveloped smiling muscles at the corners of the mouth. If you suspect shyness, say quietly that you know it will take time for you both to get to know one another, but you want to go ahead anyway. If you are shy too, say so. It is always worth knowing ignore types really well. They are witty, charming company, and good conversationalists. Once accepted, you are a friend for life.

THE 'RESCUED' TYPE

Some parents get their children to rescue them – we saw earlier that this produces 'rescuers' who have the self-sacrifice reaction when depressed. Rescuers are not likely to threaten you. But there are also parents who control their children by doing too much for them – 'Let me do that, dear, you know you always make a mess of it'; or, 'Poor darling – is Mummy not helping you?' – and these kids turn into people who can pose a very real threat by trying to make you rescue them. They are called 'rescueds'. The underlying tragedy of the severely rescued child is that it is not allowed to grow up. It can get its own way by being a grown baby, that is to say, by having a tantrum when thwarted, by being weak and helpless, by always demanding the impossible, or by simply expecting love and affection without ever understanding that these two kinds of fruit do not grow on trees. Of course, every baby with normal human luck can get itself spoiled by somebody, so there tends to be a bit of the pampered child in every one of us, prepared to look and sound helpless when it pays us, and to let others run around after us. When other people do this to you it can make you feel manipulated, used, and frustrated, and heading for crisis.

To spot those most likely to do this, look for two signs. The first is an ability to tell marvellous stories about trivial happenings. This type provides most of the 'drama kings' or 'drama queens' of the world, and in their hands, even the routine purchase of a ticket on a bus can become a hilarious or gripping adventure. The teller is always the centre of the story, too, whether it is tragic or comic. But there are few jokes as such – rescued types can very rarely remember the punch lines, and are funny when telling jokes more because they get them wrong than because the actual jokes are funny. Secondly, look for the signs of the 'grown-up' baby – a tendency to use baby-talk, for example, an ability to look several years younger, a pair of huge eyes, a physique like a ballet dancer or a face like a film star, a morbid preoccupation with the signs of ageing, a need to be surrounded by admirers, a voice which can go from a caress to a whine in a split second. The rescued type is all caress or drama, a fireworks display of vocal cord virtuosity accompanied by a veritable spectacle of facial flexibility. Gestures are graceful arabesques, the body drapes itself like a model who knows that a photographer is ready and waiting, and the voice is that of the professional teller of fairy tales, never dull for one moment, always changing and captivating – except when the person is upset. Then he or she pouts, flings the body around recklessly like a rag doll, and whines, or scratches everybody in earshot with the voice of the spoiled child.

Rescueds are highly manipulative. They twist you round their little finger and try to make you feel that you are being given a favour by being allowed to help them. They reward you with bit parts in their own life-dramas. They are often almost entirely without principles or ethics. 'I want' means 'I need', and 'I need' means 'I must have it at any price, as long as somebody else pays for it.' If they can't talk you into doing favours, they try to make you feel guilty. You are there to worry about them, and this means that every time they need you it tends to be a matter of life and death.

With the extreme rescueds, it really is. They get into scrapes, excruciating love tangles, debt, complicated surgery, or they get drunk, stoned, or hooked on illegal substances, and you are expected to bail them out as soon as you have stopped being cross. Then they expect you to forgive them. They assure you, hand on heart, that they will never do it again, and if you challenge this, they ask disarmingly: 'Would I lie to you?' Nevertheless you have a sneaky feeling that they will do it again – and soon. Often you know for a fact that they are already planning to do it again! What is more, they are already thinking up the next set of excuses. Who is it on your list that this description reminds you of?

Rescueds are all feelings – happy-go-lucky people who are totally involved in being, who never seem to think about doing anything that is boring or ordinary or purposeful, and who make little or no effort to provide for themselves because Dame Fortune will help out sooner or later. Life would be dull indeed without them, but they can provide the ultimate in heart-break.

DEALING WITH RESCUED TYPES

The key to understanding this type is to recognize that you are supposed to feel bad whenever you refuse to rescue them. If you avoid them, they will try to make you feel guilty and worried about what they will do next – either they will be ill, or get into worse trouble, or tell everybody what a nasty person you are. You will be the villain in the next instalment of their life-drama. This can be particularly difficult if any of the rescueds on your list are addicts. It has to be said that of all the three types, rescueds are most likely to become addicted. What should you do if somebody important on your list is an addict?

I know this is tough advice, but sooner or later you will do best to draw the line, and leave it at that. Cut off all contact – no matter what anybody thinks, and no matter what your relationship is: to be the parent of an addict can be sheer hell. You will pay a high price in your next few depressive crises, but then you will start to recover. You are better off without them, particularly if they are cynically using you by milking you dry of everything from money to hope. But if you decide to do this – and it can be the only choice they may leave you with – remember that a bit of you might want to compete with them for the star role of tragic loser. Get help from an independent counsellor with professional experience of addicts to sort out why it is *you* got hooked on rescuing. Remember that rescueds exploit your need to be a perfect parent, deputy parent, or pseudo-parent, and until you give up this impossible task you will not see an end to their impossible behaviour.

Of course, the addicts are extreme examples of the type, but in any case you will not find it easy to use avoidance tactics on anybody who belongs to this group. The reason is that they often get us to rescue them against our will by making us hide our feelings in case we look hypocritical – the 'moral blackmail' method. If we try to avoid them, we know they will be telling all and sundry what terrible people we are. Many of us, for example, have parents who live alone. They protest pitifully that they don't want help, but we know they expect it – so we get blackmailed into dropping everything and doing the rescue act because we do not want the world to know that we would rather neglect them. The 'rescued' neighbours whom we help, and who capitalize on this, benefit from the fact that we don't want everybody to see us as bad neighbours. And most of us have probably been stuck at some time or other with helping a colleague of the opposite sex for our own, hidden sexual reasons. Of course, we would not want to admit this, so we get blackmailed into doing more than we want to. In all such cases, we have to weigh the cost of being shown up as hypocrites against the need to stop being depressed. My own view is that it is better to be seen as a hypocrite.

A better alternative, however, is confrontation. Don't try to wait for the 'right time' – it will never arrive. Just show your anger as soon as you become impatient, and follow it up with the offer of some kind of 'trade'. You can expect an over-reaction – this type is expert at making you feel you have gone too far. But use only a little anger – undershoot rather than go over the top. Be prepared to feel ashamed of yourself for showing anger to a helpless old person, an unfortunate neighbour, or a misunderstood but attractive colleague – and learn how to live with this. Why feel ashamed for long? You know by now where the feeling comes from, and you can manage without it. You will not turn into a monster just because you decide to be selfish for once.

And as soon as you can, offer to do a deal. The kind that works best consists of spelling out which duties you intend to carry out in future, and which you will no longer do, in return for spending more time with the person, actually enjoying his or her company and having fun. Often it is enough simply to spell out that you recognize that the other person's life is probably boring, and to say that you want to be a real friend, not one who keeps pretending to be a good companion whilst inwardly begrudging the time this takes. Try to avoid apologizing, and don't let the other person apologize too much, either. 'Sorry' is a magic word to this type; it will be used to put a spell on you so you can be twisted around that little finger again.

The golden rule is 'never rescue a rescued'. So if you decide to build a closer, more mutual relationship, do this by shared fun rather than serious conversation – otherwise you will be tempted into offering sympathy and get drawn into the life-drama once more. The serious thing you can do is to try to increase the other person's independence. Never do a favour without also trying to help the person learn a new skill. Rescued types were often prevented from learning as children – mum or dad took over and did it all for them, and the same control method was probably used in their marriage, so they often lack basic knowledge as to how practical things work – rent books, credit cards, bank accounts, fuseboxes, car engines, central heating, and so on. Many a 'rescued' man who has been lately left alone literally does not know how to boil an egg – so explain how, and help him do it for himself. Never go all maternal and try to save time by doing it yourself. Find out what the person wants to learn by asking openly and caringly, and give very simple instructions, with plenty of practice; use lots of patience, but do not take over. Remember – the parent of this person used to say 'Let me do it, you'll only make a mess of it.' Avoid becoming either a deputy parent or a pseudo-parent. When you leave, say, 'I'm sure you'll manage – good luck!' and not, 'If you need any more help you only have to ask.' With rescueds the motto is: never apologize, always explain.

MIXTURES

This has been a long chapter, with plenty for you to take in and study, but it still falls short of a complete set of answers. The main reason is that many of the people who threaten you will be mixtures, and I have only had space to give you notes about the three main types. If in doubt, just respond to the particular control being used; for example, if somebody is a mixture of squasher and ignored, and, when you counter-squash, he looks surprised and then walks out, you should let him go, and try to do a deal with him when he comes back.

To make the best use of this whole approach, you have to read between the lines a little, and try to get a 'feel' for the way the person you wish to influence was brought up. Then, if you wish to use avoidance, try to think of how that person's parents would have used rejection, and try to be even better at it than they were. To use confrontation, act as the deputy parent – attempting to use the very same controls the parent used. As for trading, this is easiest if you completely disregard the person's parental controls, and act more as a stranger.

The best way in the long run with every type, however, is sincerely to build mutual trust, and you may have noticed that I recommend using confrontation and trading mainly as a way of opening up the possibilities of achieving this. This is particularly important with people you value, or with whom there is no choice but to share a large part of your life – although the two of you might have to start as if you were both strangers again, setting aside all the history of pseudo-parenting you have been through in the past, and this is very difficult to do.

Empathy, however, is impossible if you act in a parental, deputy or pseudo-parental way. It is the very opposite of parent-power, and can only be effective if you try actively to be a more encouraging parent to the other person than his or her parents could ever have been in childhood. Empathy depends on loving somebody a little bit more – even if you don't like that person – and it is far and away the best method of reducing any threat. Love, in the sense of giving somebody free gifts of energy, space, and time, is the only thing ultimately that casts out fear and anger on both sides – and here I speak as a scientist. You'll see what I mean later.

Chapter Ten

HOW CAN YOU START TO FEEL BETTER?

NO INSTANT IMMUNITY

The best way to start fighting depression is to take the initiative with people who make you feel threatened and get them to treat you differently. However, this by itself can not guarantee instant immunity from self-attack. In this chapter we shall consider why this is so, and then go on to discuss how you can also change yourself from the inside – delaying crises, having fewer of them, and lessening their impact when they occur.

There are several reasons why you are still likely to have periods of deep depression for quite a long time. First, there is a lot to learn – about the people in your life who trigger your attacks, about the different kinds of triggers they use, and about the tactics which are most likely to be effective when you first start using the ACTE method. Many of these ideas are new to you, and you may not understand them fully without reading some chapters several times – and, in any case, you may not be able to accept all of it at once. I have concentrated a lot on the part played by parents in making us vulnerable to depression, and at least three generations of propaganda in favour of parent-power and against the basic notions of psychotherapy stand between you and this set of truths, as well as the opinions of people who favour brain chemistry and genetics as the explanation for the illness. It might take you a long time to realize exactly what your parents did to you, to accept that this was wrong, and to see that this still affects you every day of your life.

Secondly, you need practice at using the methods, and you need to make mistakes that you can learn from. Now, when I refer to practice, I don't mean that you will have to find half a dozen people to act out the part of threatener while you rehearse your lines. The only guinea pigs you have are the real people in your life who threaten you today, or who will threaten you tomorrow. You have to try the methods out on them – and in real life, as you know, it is easy to fail, and easy to feel discouraged. Your depression is not going to surrender meekly the first time you try to defeat it, just as your parents would not have caved in at the first sign of resistance from you if you stood up to them when you were little. Indeed, if your power struggles with them were long and bitter, you can expect a long and bitter fight with depression. Your present struggle is, after all, a continuation of the same campaign, except that this time you can win, whereas last time you couldn't. But you won't win without a fight.

Thirdly, some of the people in your life are not going to be too happy about you avoiding them, standing up to them, being cheeky enough to offer them deals as if you were an equal, or suggesting that the two of you might get to know one another better. As long as deputy and pseudo-parents have power over you – even if they are unaware of this – they stand to gain from your depression, and so when you start to take power away from them, they are not likely to welcome this. Of course, if they care about you they will encourage you – but this will mean they have to learn some new lessons too, and this takes time. Also, most of us are close to at least one person who claims to care, and whose ability to care, when put to the test, will not be what it seems. So you can expect to see some people for the first time for what they really are instead of what you hoped they were, and this by itself can be depressing.

However, there are advantages that begin to stack up in your favour once you begin to change the way others treat you. For a start, a lot of people will begin to see you in a different light. Those who really do care about you – and there may be more of them than you think – will welcome the change in your behaviour, even if they find you difficult to live with. After all, they are quite used to this. But now you will come across as much more positive, much better able to stick up for yourself, and that means you will be more exciting for them to have around.

Once you have started to prove to yourself that this really

works – and it won't work unless you take the risk and try it out – something else will begin to happen. This is that you will not only be seen differently by other people – you will also begin to see yourself as different. At first, of course, it will only be your actions which alter. You will remain the same person inside, and feel just the same way about yourself. At times you will have to behave somewhat artificially, like somebody acting a part. Indeed, it can take a long time to get through this 'rehearsal' period and begin to 'live' the new role you have written for yourself. But the fact that people will begin to respond differently towards you will little by little make it much harder for you not to change yourself.

Why is this? The reason is that whenever two people make contact they expect certain things of one another, and, as a result they modify their own behaviour so that what they expect to happen will be more likely to happen. An example will help to illustrate what I mean. Suppose somebody thinks of you as shy and reserved. This will make him talk to you 'in your own language', as if he were shy too. He will tend to suppress his own need to show off, and behave in a rather more cautious way with you than if he thought of you as a loud and boastful person. The result is that he gives you very few opportunities in conversation to contradict his view of you. He gets used to treating you as shy, and you begin to turn into the person he expects you to be – at least, you turn into this kind of person each time the two of you meet. However, you might behave quite differently with somebody else who thinks of you as not shy at all. People treat you according to the kinds of assumptions they make about you, and this sets limits on the ways you can behave when you are with them.

Now, when you start to change the way other people treat you, they begin to give you all sorts of opportunities to be this new kind of person. And they don't only give you the ones you have worked hard to get. They start to offer you openings to be the person you want to be because this makes sense for them too. Having changed their view of you, they can see no point in *not* treating you the way you seem to want to be treated. All these new chances make it very hard for you not to change for real. So if you used to come across as one of the world's natural victims, and people used to take advantage, once you have made them see you in a different light they will not only stop trying to take advantage of you, but behave in a more generous way towards you generally – telling you more, laughing with you more, treating you as one of them. It is one of the facts of human behaviour that whenever we find we like somebody, we start to treat them as if they are like us. The effect of all this is that you will start to turn into the new you almost inevitably and gradually forget your former self.

As we have seen, however, during that awkward ugly duckling phase when you are having to act a part with some people, you will still have periods of depression. The crises will not have gone away just yet. They may come a little less often, but at first they will be just as bad as ever – that is to say they will last just about as long, or feel just about as bad. So what we need to do next is look at how you can lessen the impact of those crises which are still going to occur.

DELAYING THE ONSET OF CRISIS

The first question to ask yourself is whether you can delay an attack of the miseries. The advantages of doing so are fairly obvious. It will enable you to avoid going into the 'down' at times when those who provoked it might be in a very strong position to exploit your misery. For example, if a threat from a parent causes you to be self-violent while the parent is still there, this might encourage him or her to push home the advantage and make matters worse, whereas, if you can hang on till the parent has gone, this will be less likely to happen. Delaying your reaction can also help you to put off an attack of despair long enough for those who care about you but who might not have been there when the threat occurred, to help you out of it more effectively later. For example, being 'squashed' by some stranger and feeling bad about it might make you suicidal at the time, but if you can delay the feeling, and talk about it to a friend, you will feel better. Or you might be able to delay a crisis long enough for the feelings to 'go away of their own accord', so you avoid that particular crisis altogether.

How can you delay a crisis? Oddly enough, one of the most important things you can do is listen much more carefully to the kinds of things you say when you are close to a crisis. Never mind why – the reasons are too complex to explain just yet – but almost all of us start to broadcast our distress before we actually feel it. We start to say things which tell those with ears to hear that we are just about to go into a 'down'. If we listen to ourselves say these things – and if we can recruit people who care about us to help do the same thing – we can often become aware of the attack of deep depression in time to be able to control it. Let me give you some examples.

Remember right at the beginning, when I discussed the sort of things depressed people say to the doctor? I gave three examples: 'I expect you'll think it is all wrong'; 'It's silly I know'; and 'I know it's ridiculous.' Just before we have a 'down' nearly all of us start to come out with an increasing number of phrases like this which use the word 'it'. Not surprisingly, they are called 'it-statements'.

Now, the importance of these statements is that they carry more than one message – indeed, they are sometimes called 'double messages'. The first and most obvious part of the message refers to something outside the speaker. But in a subtle way, and often without realizing what we are doing, we are also letting other people know how we feel inside. We are using the word 'it' in two ways – first to stand for an object or situation, and second to refer to ourselves. That is to say, in the second part of the message we are using the word 'it' where we mean 'I'.

In the example above, the person was saying, first, that he expected the doctor to think that what he was about to say would be 'all wrong'. But secondly, he was referring to himself and saying that *he* was all wrong. In the next example, the speaker was saying not only that the situation was silly, but also that he or she was silly. The third was telling the doctor on the one hand that being depressed is ridiculous, and on the other hand, telling the world that he or she – the patient –was ridiculous. Let's look at some more examples to show you what I mean.

'It's a hopeless mess.' 'That's no good at all.' 'It's not what I want.' 'It's selfish, but . . .' In each case there is one message which describes something in the speaker's outside world – thus, the 'hopeless mess' referred to might be some kind of tangled situation at home or at work. And there is a second message which describes the speaker's inner world and gives us a clue as to what is going on there. In this second message, the 'hopeless mess' is the speaker himself. That is to say, 'It's a hopeless mess' means 'I am a hopeless mess.' The word 'I' has been changed into the word 'it'.

Where does this second message come from? To answer this question, we have to accept that there is a struggle going on inside the person, a struggle for self-control which, as we have seen, is a continuation of the childhood battle for parental control. In effect, the speaker is attacking himself on behalf of his parent as he tries to control his feelings. Notice that he stops being an 'I' and becomes an 'it' – an object, not a person. This shows that a power struggle is going on, because when power is used, the person with the power always stops seeing his 'victim' as a whole person, and sees him as an object instead.

We can now take our analysis a step further. From the actual words used in an it-statement, we can deduce what is being said on behalf of the parent – in effect, what that person's parent used to say to him. Look at the examples again. 'That's no good at all' is what the person is telling himself on behalf of his parent. It shows us that the speaker was probably discouraged in childhood by being told he or she was no good at all, or, at the very least, being made to feel this way – an example of the squashing parent's way of putting the child down. If this is true, there will be other evidence to support it. 'It's not what I want' means, 'I am not what is wanted,' so the parent in this case used to say, 'You are not what I want,' and the child knew that 'I am not what my parent wanted.' This 'unwanted child' was very probably an ignored child, and will almost certainly show this in other ways, too. Using the same kind of detective work, the last example tells us that the parent used to say: 'You are selfish,' and you will already know by now that this is typical of the parent who produces a rescuer child. Again, if this is true, then there will be supporting evidence.

If you listen to yourself, and look out for it-statements, you will find that you begin to give out more and more of them as you fight harder and harder for self-control. You can also listen to other people, and you will find that they do the same thing. But how can you use this idea to help yourself?

First, say out loud or in your head what you really feel by correcting the 'it' to 'I': for example, correct '*it is* a waste of time' to '*I am* a waste of time.' Next, listen to this message. Do you want to accept it as the truth about yourself? It is almost certainly one of the things your parent used to tell you in order to discourage you during a power struggle – you might remember it being said. So you can now change the message once more so it reads: 'My dad (or mum) used to think I was a waste of time.'

This is the message that really matters – the one that you have been suppressing by using an it-statement. And if you think about this one, you will see that you no longer have to believe what they used to say about you. You are not a waste of time – you are a person in your own right, just as entitled as anybody else to take all the time you need. In any case, what they said all those years ago might be an interesting historical fact, and it might make you feel very angry with them – but it need not influence you right now and it certainly need not provoke you into wanting to beat yourself up, run away, or feel guilty. You do not have to have a crisis just because they would have had one under similar circumstances. You can manage without your parent's control. In fact, you can manage your life far better now than they could ever have done. If this is what you really believe, then say it in your head. And it won't hurt you to say it out loud either. I have known a lot of depressed people who found they could fend off a crisis in this way – by actually saying out loud, 'Dad, go away and leave me alone,' or 'Mum – trust me, I can manage without you.' You can be as rude as you like, too. I find that stammerers and stutterers are particularly helped when taught to be very rude.

Listening to it-statements can give us, and people who want to help us, advance warning of our inner battles for control. This can help us delay a crisis, or manage without one. We can also listen to other people's it-statements to see what is going on inside them when they get upset. And there are other statements like this we can listen to. For example, there are 'not-statements', such as 'I'm not angry,' or 'I'm not scared,' or 'I'm not sorry,' and so on. You can try translating them whenever you hear yourself using them: 'I'm not' means 'I am trying hard not to.' Thus, 'I don't care' can often mean, 'I am trying hard not to care.' 'I don't think about that' might mean 'I am trying hard not to think about that,' and 'I'm not worried about him' is likely to mean 'I am trying hard not to worry about him.' My point is not necessarily that you should stop 'trying hard'. It is that once you know you are doing this, you can try hard with less effort.

Another example of this kind of thing is 'not really'. It very often means 'yes, a little bit'. Thus, if you are asked whether you want to go out, and you say, 'Not really' you mean, 'Yes, I would like to go out – but I feel this way only a little bit.' Or, if you are asked if you feel sad, and you say, 'Not really,' you mean that you feel sad a little bit. When people say this to me I tend to reply: 'Not really means a little bit – tell me about the little bit!' Quite often that little bit turns out to be quite a big bit. Sometimes they tell me I'm wrong, but then, you can't win 'em all.

SOFTENING THE BLOWS

It isn't always possible to delay the crisis. What can you do to help yourself if you fail? To answer this question we have to recall some of the things we said earlier about the different reactions we have when we go into a 'down'. What we do to ourselves during a depressive crisis is what our dominant parent threatened to do to us in order to control our behaviour and turn us into the kind of person he or she wanted us to be. Knowing this gives us several ways of lessening the hurtfulness of the crisis.

First, remember that when you start a crisis you are acting on behalf of the parent. When you were little you had no choice except to try to be the kind of person your parent wanted. We can put this another way round, too – you had to stop being the sort of person your parent did not want, and did not like. Today you have a choice. You can do things they could not do, you can have things they could not have, and you can be things they were not able to be. You are allowed to turn into the kind of person they would not have liked, also. This won't hurt you – there must be lots of people you like whom your parent would not have been able to tolerate. What harm will it do if you behave in a similar way to one of those people? As long as you like yourself, and the people who are important to you still like you, what does it matter if your parent would not have liked you?

Of course, you might argue that this is all very well, but you don't like yourself – you are a complete failure, an embarrassment to everybody, a selfish person who is guilty of all sorts of crimes. But is this you talking, or your parent? If it's you, then I see what you mean, and, fine, I'm sure you're right. But if it's not you, but a parental echo from way back, then you are going to have to make up your mind whether you want to listen. My advice is: don't.

Secondly, remember that parents vary a great deal in how hard they discourage their children. Picture them standing in a line, with the mild discouragers at one end and the severe ones at the opposite end. The mildest only squash, ignore, or manipulate when they are very hard pressed, and even then they apologize as soon as they can. A little bit further down the line, they squash, ignore, and get themselves rescued by the child quite often, but not very seriously. That is to say, if they slap, they do not hit hard; if they send the child away, it is sent away only for a short time; and if they make the child feel guilty, they make their point with a minimum of fuss and then give the child a cuddle so it doesn't feel that way for too long. Even further down the line, we get the parents who control the child very fiercely, but who only do this in crisis, and who try hard to make up for this when the crisis has passed. Next, there are the ones who control fiercely most of the time, and at the extremely severe end, the ones who do so all the time.

The worst things you do to yourself were the worst things that your parent threatened to do to you. Today, however, when you start to punish yourself in a depressive crisis – and you are perfectly at liberty to do so – you can try to be slightly more lenient than this. You can make your point without overdoing things. One way is to try to spend less time being violent, banishing, or sorry towards yourself. For example, instead of sentencing yourself to an hour of violence, rejection, or guilt, you can lessen the sentence to three-quarters of an hour. You can even cut it down to half an hour. Even if you are just as fierce with yourself – and you might deserve to be – then at least you can get it over with more quickly. Most of our punishments seem lighter when we can get them over and done with more quickly. Another way is to use less energy on punishment – to hit yourself, but not hit so hard, or to hit an object which won't break, or to grumble at yourself instead of hitting; to feel like running away, but walking instead, or to come back before you reach your 'place of sin'; to cry, but to keep your breathing a little more easy so that the sobs are less violent. You need to be able to tell yourself that enough is enough and, of course, to combine this with all the other methods we have talked about, so that fewer people actually benefit from you being like this.

People who are not depressed get angry sometimes, and let the feeling 'go away by itself'. You can try this too – by letting it drain away. The nearest equivalent to doing this with anger and anxiety is the way you and I probably dealt with inconvenient sexy feelings when we were teenagers – you think of something else and try to relax until the feeling subsides. There are often classes you can go to in order to learn more about relaxation and good breathing, and these will help. Some people are helped by yoga, and some by a new commitment to religious faith and meditation. Others find that a good walk works just as well – it takes your mind off things and helps you relax.

BETTER PARENTING

Depression is self-punishment on behalf of the parent, and you can do a great deal to lessen the effects of it by learning to be a better parent to yourself. But this is one of those 'easier said than done' things, so we need to spell it out in more detail. Remember the four things I suggested you should do towards the other people in your life who make you feel threatened? They were avoidance, confrontation, doing a deal (trading), and the empathy method: ACTE. Each one of these should be used not just on other people, but on yourself.

Avoidance in this context means not spending so much energy, space, and time on hurting yourself, as I have just explained. Confrontation means standing up to the parent in your head, using the it-statements, and the other coded messages the way I described earlier. Doing a deal with yourself means giving yourself permission to turn into the kind of person you want to be by promising the parent in your head that you will manage without troubling him or her. Self-empathy means using everything I have written in this book to get to know yourself better and to start to trust yourself more.

So there's quite a lot you can do to start feeling better once you have begun to get other people to change their attitude towards you. It will take you a very long way in the direction of a permanent cure. But to go the whole way we need to understand what we mean by cure.

Chapter Eleven

CAN YOU CURE YOUR DEPRESSION?

WHAT KIND OF AN ILLNESS?

Cure and recovery generally mean returning to the same state of health we had before we were ill. We talk about somebody 'recovering his health', 'being herself again', or 'getting back to normal'. Of course, there are some conditions from which people do not recover. They might have an 'incurable illness' – one where the cause is unknown, or the cure has not yet been found. Or they might have a 'disability', that is to say, their bodies lack something which most other people's bodies have, so they need permanent help to counteract this deficiency. In terms of our chances of recovery, what kind of illness is depression?

The answer is that it does not fit into any of these categories. Recovery from depression cannot mean returning to a former, better state of health. If depression arises directly from grieving, then this is because the good times are gone for ever. And if grief of some kind is not the immediate cause, then discouragement is, and the sufferer has never known anything but discouragement. In other words, recovery in the ordinary sense of going back to a former state is out of the question. But at the same time, we should not regard depression as a disability – we can, but it would be wrong to do so. Disabilities can be eased by enabling people to cope, but those who are coping with depression are actually ill with depression, so helping them to cope will only keep them ill, and in any case, the only medical way of helping them to cope appears to be to encourage a life-long dependence on anti-depressants, and that is no answer at all. It is also unhelpful to regard depression as an incurable mental illness. To see it this way inevitably means treating sufferers as needing to be permanently protected from themselves, to be judged and blamed, pitied and patronized. We end up adding more discouragement to an already intolerable history of discouragement. Surely that is not the answer, either.

The fact is, depression is not the kind of illness where cure means going back to a former state of health. It is one of a group of illnesses where recovery can only mean ending up *better* than you have ever been before. To be cured of depression you have to attain a standard of health which will be an improvement on anything you have ever previously known.

But what does this mean? First of all it means we have to abandon the naïve idea that 'health' is the mere absence of illness. As long as we think in these terms we shall never understand depression. Secondly, it means that being cured of depression is impossible unless you can change into the kind of person you have never been before – not just the way you are now plus a little more happiness, but the kind of person you have only ever dreamed of becoming, somebody whose capability is quite different – the person you would have been if you hadn't been discouraged in childhood.

MINI-ECONOMY

If this sounds impossible at first, it is just that most of us are not used to thinking of any illness in this way. And the reason for this is basically because we still divide illnesses into physical and mental illness. For centuries we have thought of each person consisting of three separate parts – body, mind, and soul – each of which can be 'sick' separately. Depression cannot be understood in these terms. It is neither a 'physical' nor a 'mental' illness, nor a physical, mental, or spiritual disability. To cure it we have to take a different tack altogether, and bring our ideas about health into line with other modern scientific ideas.

The way to understand people is to see each individual as a living system, where the word 'system' is used in its scientific sense of something whole and complete, where what happens to each part inevitably affects all the other parts. The 'system' idea is one we are all used to – think of the solar system, or systems such as a rain-forest, or the environment generally. Every part of a system depends for its well-being on all the other parts. This applies to humans too. Each man, woman, or child is a complete organism, a whole system, dependent in many ways on other systems, but nevertheless a system in its own right.

But the important point is not just that each of us is a system. What matters is that each one of us is a special kind of system – one that is made up of a multitude of resources, all of which can be co-ordinated and managed to meet the needs of the whole. Every person is, in effect, a mini-economy, though I prefer the more accurate term, 'psycho-economy'. To put it simply, we each have our own unique needs; we also have our own unique set of resources; and the task we face each moment of our lives is to use those resources in order to meet our needs.

Don't be put off by the word 'economy' – you understand it well enough. All it means is that to meet our needs we have to have enough resources. If we don't have enough resources, we cannot meet our needs and we become worse off. If we have resources to spare, we have choice in our lives. We've all used this idea since childhood – we learned about it when we spent our pocket money as children, and we live with it all the time as home managers or bread-winners. Yet here I am not just talking about money. Money is only one kind of human resource. There are many other kinds – strength, agility, endurance, skills and abilities, memory, past experience and intelligence, land and property, clothes, cars, and homes, the people we share our lives with, the benefits we obtain by being citizens, and so on.

As soon as we recognize that each person is a system, we can see at once what being ill is, what coping is, and why coping is not the same as being healthy. We become ill when our resources are not enough to meet our needs – or as an accountant would say, when we are in deficit, or overdrawn. We can cope when our resources exactly meet our needs and no more – at the break-even point. But to be healthy we need to have surplus resources – more than will be necessary to meet our immediate requirements. Only then can we have a full and healthy life, with plenty of real choices about how we live.

The problem when we suffer from depression is that we

never have a surplus with which to grow, for we are stuck with either coping or being in deficit. Every human system is under threat if it can only break even, or if it is in deficit. We only have to look at our everyday experience to see this. We all know how desperately hard it is to make choices when we can only just 'cope' financially, because then everything we have is spoken for before we get it. We are trapped. True, we can survive, but we cannot hope for anything better, and any small savings we manage to make are totally inadequate the moment somebody makes new demands upon us. The same is true when we can only just cope emotionally. Remember how Jean felt in the story? Her husband came home that Friday, and the demands on her whole system shot up, increasing way past the point she had budgeted for, and wiping out all her 'savings' so she had less than nothing left to spare. That is what a set-back is: a sudden increase in the demands made on our systems so our savings are wiped out.

When we are in deficit, quite simply our lives are not our own. If we are physically helpless, emotionally in turmoil, lonely, and unable to meet any of our own needs, then the people with power over us – the ones we are forced to depend on – make all our choices for us, and they usually make them so that their needs take priority over ours. Unless we can get the resources from somewhere to change this, we have to play life their way, just to stay alive. We are forced to obey impatient commands from squashers, to live on the meagre hand-outs of attention the ignorers deign to give us when they get round to it, or endlessly to try to please the manipulative rescueds by making acts of self-sacrifice they never thank us for.

But if we have a surplus, we can grow by investing the extra, and that is the whole point of using ACTE. We can spend some of our resources avoiding people – people who want to take our resources away from us or make us waste them. We can use some of our surplus through confrontation to make others give us what we are entitled to. We can trade with people, using some of the surplus so as to swap poor conditions for better ones. We can give some of our resources away without counting the cost in that age-old human custom called love.

There is only one cure for depression, and that is for you to create a surplus of your own – energy and space and time won back from those who want it for themselves at cost to you, surplus resources which you can use for yourself to take charge of your own growth, and to determine at last how much power, how much trading, and how much love there will be in your own life. You have never done it before, you say? But you can do it if you want to. And you have always wanted to. It's just that every time you've tried it, somebody has triggered a depressive crisis in you and you have been unable to defend the gains you have made.

PROFIT CENTRES

To cure depression you will need to get past coping and start to grow again, and that means having more resources in your system than you can recall ever having had before. You will have to find quite a lot of these for yourself, although some of them will come from loving, caring people as interest-free loans. What we need to ask now is this: what kinds of resources do you need to have more of, and how can you get them? It would be nice to tell you in detail – and I shall try to do this – but if you can take on board one more idea, I shall explain the principle which is involved, so you can devise new ideas for yourself.

Because each one of us is a resource system with needs, we are similar to all other such systems. A modern business is one of the systems we resemble. Today, a great many of the most successful companies are organized into what are called 'profit centres'. Each of these is like a division of the main company, and it has to try to make its own surplus. The managers in charge of the whole company have the task of keeping an eye on each profit centre, and making sure that if one of them makes a loss, resources are switched around from the profitable sectors to support it and get it to start growing again. Of course, it isn't a new idea. Every good home manager knows how to save a bit on the food to find the extra for clothes, and so on, but this is never called 'profit centre management'!

Each one of us has four main divisions: the body, which consists of our physical resources; the behavioural system, which is made up of all the things we have ever learned to do; the property system, comprising all the things we own; and the social system, containing the benefits we get from knowing people privately or from belonging to groups. The condition we call health is what happens when each of these profit centres is able to deliver a surplus, and when the 'management' – that is you – can use the extra to enhance your own standard of life through power, trading, and love. The principle you need to follow is this: act as a good manager of your whole system. That means not letting other people take over, though obviously you should let them help if they really love you and give you their resources freely and with no strings attached. It also means getting your own 'expenditure' under control, and cutting down where you can so you can build up your 'savings'.

But remember that if one division produces a deficit, the surplus from another division automatically gets used to pay it off. For example, if the things people demand from you are too difficult, even if you are physically fit, your body has to pay for this by using everything it has saved. As these automatic subsidies continue, the strain can become too great for it to bear, and you become physically ill with no apparent physical cause – what is called a 'psychosomatic' illness. People can become physically ill for economic reasons too – the poor are always those with the worst physical health all over the world. Social deficits such as loneliness or feeling unattractive can also drain away physical health, and make you physically ill. So you have to try to keep all four divisions fit and happy and in surplus at the same time, and at the very least to keep one in surplus if the rest can only break even. Let me explain in more detail.

PHYSICAL SURPLUS

A physical surplus is the most important of all. See that you get enough sleep, enough exercise, that you get your weight right, that your diet is healthy, that you use some of your energy every day to make space and time where you can relax and pamper yourself.

I know that none of this is easy, but the methods I have already described should make it easier, and the fact is, next to a phone call from a parent your worst enemy is fatigue. We all get 'downs' more often when we are tired than at any other time. We run ourselves short of the physical resources we need, and the result is that we are forced to subsidize our bodies by lowering the value of our other resources. We don't just feel bad physically, we begin to think of ourselves as worthless. We stop enjoying the things we own. And we reject those who love us.

BEHAVIOURAL SURPLUS

You also have to try to keep a 'behavioural surplus' – that is to say, to be able as far as possible to have choices about what you can do in any situation. If your work does not give you this, either try to reorganize it so that it does – by using ACTE on the people who control it – or give it up and do something else. If you are going through a bad patch, do as little as you can until you feel better. Doing nothing is better than trying to do the impossible.

Try not to be afraid of indecision. You will find that as you grow stronger you will be able to decide what to do next. Remember also that taking a break from work helps to solve every kind of problem – provided the resources you gain are not immediately annexed by somebody who wants to use you for his or her own purposes, and provided you do not spend them on hurting yourself. Again, the methods I have already described will help. Protect your right to take a break and to recover from pressure by using ACTE.

Outside work, build up a behavioural surplus by learning new skills and developing your own creativity. A new skill can be anything you would like to do but have never done – from mending a fuse to reading music. Creativity means learning to write bad poems, paint terrible pictures, make awful music, cook uneatable but original meals, and bit by bit learning to do all such things better. Take lessons or join a group. Remember: do it badly first. Do it better next. Save up doing it perfectly until last. And always defend your right to grow and learn and make mistakes, particularly against people with parent-power who profit from your discouragement. It is their kind who restricted your creativity in childhood and this time you must not let them get away with it.

PROPERTY SURPLUS

Property resources are very important. The most obvious of these is money. Try to be independent if you can – I know it isn't easy, but see what you can do. For example, if you are married, a joint bank account is a good idea, but having a joint account, together with each of you having a separate account is even better. It will help you feel that you have something of your own, and this may be a new feeling. Insist that what is in there is yours. See if you can increase what you earn, and put the extra into your own account, even if you have to take it out again. At least you will feel it belonged to you, and that you are capable of deciding how to spend it.

The less obvious property resources are also important. You will soon exhaust yourself if the equipment you need is not fitted to its purpose. Make sure at least that your bed will not keep you awake, that your usual chair is comfy, that your lavatory is a cosy place to sit, and that cleaning and cooking utensils are not more trouble than they are worth. If you are desperately short of money, try to learn how to scavenge and scrounge for things that are better than yours but which others do not want. Turn it into a skill, particularly if your parents would have been horrified at such undignified behaviour, or have taught you to be too proud to behave this way. The same applies to clothes, too – second-hand is 'in'!

Whenever you can, buy yourself a present. A present is something you want, not because you need it, or because it is worth having, but as a reward for being you. It is your reward to yourself, and nobody's business but your own. Avoid false presents which are ironic rewards – the things which put you down. Booze is a good example. Too much of it will degrade rather than enhance you. Cream cakes if you are overweight are bad too – reward your best self, not your hurt self. By the way, the nearest park is a property resource you own by being a citizen, so reward yourself by going out for a walk and just enjoying it.

SOCIAL SURPLUS

There are two kinds of social resource – public ones and private ones. Public resources are important. You need to feel that you belong to organizations and neighbourhoods, and to meet new people you can help and who can help you. Being happy and busy and having fun with other people is one of the best ways there is of combating depression. The energy people give you back, the skills you learn from them, and the joy that comes from using things you could not afford yourself – all these will help you grow. The old suggestions, to 'get out and enjoy yourself', or to join an evening class, are still good answers to depression.

If you have been lonely for a long time getting out will take courage. If you are shy, talking to strangers will be very hard work at first. Pick on people who look safe and happy – couples, people older than you, busy people, shop-keepers – and say hello. Save the difficult people, the very attractive ones, till you have had more practice at chatting. But make some new relationships – with strangers, and with the people who used to think they knew you.

WHERE TO CONCENTRATE

Of course, most of this is the kind of good advice you will have heard before. The difference this time is that I am not suggesting you follow it piecemeal, but that you see it as a starting point for systematically taking charge of your life. If you understand what was done to you, and want to put things right, then there is no reason why you cannot become a better self-manager. This is what I meant at the start when I talked about neutralizing the causes of depression. To do this you have to set out deliberately to become the person your parents could not let you be when you were a child. Imagine what it would be like if all the bullied, neglected, and manipulated kids in the world had a revolution and kicked their parents out. That is what I'm suggesting, only it just isn't possible until each of those children has grown up. So now is the time for a revolution in your life. Put them and their deputies out of business. You can do a better job of managing yourself now than they ever could.

Concentrate on building up those surpluses – and you don't necessarily have to start with the physical ones, either. Tackle it any way which is easy for you. If your main reaction is self-violence, you probably have enough physical resources already – you certainly do not seem short of them each time you attack yourself. Save more by attacking yourself less. Your main deficit is much more likely to be behavioural – you will think of yourself as rather short on skills, so tackle this last. Begin by getting your economy right – acquire more money and property – then make some new friends by learning to be a better listener, and only after that concentrate on building new skills. Have a go at being a squasher, instead of being squashed. Then learn the skills of the ignorer and the rescuer so you become one of life's all-rounders.

If you are mainly a self-banisher, then you run the risk of being too clever and too isolated. Just being ordinary and making some new, real friends will be quite difficult for you, so save this till you're a bit better. Start by getting your body right. Then get out and about and show it off in some new clothes. Try to be a noisier ignore type, rather than the quiet kind. You have it in you to be the sort of person everybody will admire, so once they start doing so, let them, and polish up your creative and performance skills in order to please them even more. You can do it – they've seen nothing yet!

If you are the rescuer type – inclined to say please, sorry, thank you, and excuse me for your own life, then you will already be very good with people, but tend to neglect your body. You probably have had more diets than the rest of us have had hot dinners! So don't start in either of those places. Your best bet is to learn some new skills, to let others do the teaching, and to turn the skills into a new source of income you can spend on yourself. You will only have to be selfish for a while – once you have something to keep, you will have more to give, and more choice about whom you give it to. You too need to become better at ignoring and squashing. So have fun being the boss and the expert for a change, instead of being the servant.

LETTING OTHERS HELP

Depressed people are amongst the hardest people in the world to help. As I said earlier, this is because we each have a tendency to be depressed, and a worse tendency in somebody else makes us feel more depressed. But there is no doubt that trying to defeat depression without the help of somebody else is very difficult – a long hard road which it will take years to travel. When we were children we would not have been hurt half as much if we had had somebody we could always rely on to love us whatever we did, without terms and conditions, and that is what we most need now. But it isn't any easier to obtain now than it was then, and depression can make it more difficult.

If you have somebody who really cares about you, the two of you need to team up and to tackle depression together – thinking of it as something you have jointly, not as one of you having it and the other one helping. You are not victim and helper, but two victims together, helping each other. Try to keep a surplus for each other, and when one of you runs out of resources and the inevitable depressive crisis sets in, the other partner can help to get it over with more quickly. Always encourage one another. And what you cannot do together, try to do individually whilst staying together. If sex is out as far as your partner is concerned – and it often is when one of you gets depressed – get your partner to cuddle you and be sexy for yourself. It's very easy to use lack of sex as a stick to beat yourself or your partner with – some of us had parents who never wanted us to be sexual. But there is more to sex than the mechanics, and whatever you do, you can help both of you best by showing tenderness.

Perhaps the hardest thing to do if you live with somebody who is depressed is to stay calm and useful during those agonies of self-hurt, whether they come out as threats of suicide, or as constant self-doubt and self-denigration. Remember that this happens when the person you want to help is unable to feel committed to life, and that even if the threat which triggered off this rejection of life seems out of proportion to you, the chances are that it is being under-stated, not exaggerated. Respond to the threat the depressed person feels – not to the one you feel. And remember that you yourself may be threatening in ways you have never realized, and that even if you do not mean to be a threat, this will not make the people you threaten feel any better. So get to work on yourself, too.

When either of you feels down, you have to try to avoid having a power struggle in which you take over as pseudo-parent, or you go into a crisis yourself. The danger of simultaneous crisis is that when it happens, neither of you can help the other, so try to avoid this by keeping some resources put by for one another in case a crisis strikes. To help anybody through depression you have to try at all times to be one of the genuine reasons for that person to want to stay alive, and to grow again. Maybe that is what all of us should try to do all the time for everybody.

But of course it isn't simple. If curing depression were simple, the world would be a totally different place, not just for those of us who suffer from it at first hand, but for everybody else, too. But there is much you can do short of a cure to reduce your vulnerability to this awful scourge. At the very least, you can make up your mind to ask for help – from those who love you, and, if there is nobody, from a skilled helper who will be on your side and not judge you and find you wanting. There need be no shame in taking this first step. Your depression is not your fault. But it is your responsibility, and shouldering the burden now may one day lighten that heavy load you have carried for so long.

APPENDIX

COUNSELLING FOR DEPRESSION: USEFUL ADDRESSES

Public libraries are an excellent source of information on local groups and national organizations of all kinds – all you need do is ask at the desk.

British Association for Counselling
37a Sheep St, Rugby, Warwicks
CV21 3AP
(0788–73241)
Has a register of accredited counsellors and will give contact information for those in your area.

British Association of Psychotherapists
121 Hendon Lane, London N3
(01–346–1747)

Cruse Head Office
Cruse House, 126 Sheen Rd, Richmond, Surrey TW9 1UR
(01–940–4818)
Helps to arrange bereavement counselling.

Depressives Anonymous
83 Derby Rd, Nottingham NG1 5BB
Puts you in touch with self-help groups.

MIND (National Association for Mental Health)
22 Harley St, London W1N 2ED
(01–637–0741)
Has local groups in many districts. Full information about its services is available from head office.

Samaritans Head Office
17 Uxbridge Rd, Slough SL1 1SN
(0753–32713)
For local services see telephone directory. Can help during acute crises and offers confidential, ongoing assistance to those fighting depression.

Westminster Pastoral Foundation
23 Kensington Square, London W8 5HN
(01–937–6956)
For group and individual therapy and counselling.

Women's Therapy Centre
19a Hartman Rd, London N7
*Group and individual therapy for
  women only.*

MORE SPECIALIZED HELP

Action Against Allergy
43, The Downs, London SW20 8HG
(01–947–5082)

Albany Trust
(01–730–5871)
*Helps people, especially members
  of sexual minorities, who have
  psycho-sexual worries.*

Alcoholics Anonymous
11 Redcliffe Gardens, London
  SW10 9BG
(01–352–9779)
*For details of assistance outside
  London.*

Alcoholics Anonymous
140a Tachbrook St, London
  SW1V 2NE
For callers in London.

Association of Sexual and Marital
  Therapists
PO Box 62, Sheffield S10

Bassanio Trust
35, Woodberry Way, London
  N12 0HE
(01–445–0581)
*Helps those in trouble with the law
  through stress and depression –
  London and Southern England.*

Portia Trust
15, Senhouse St, Maryport,
  Cumbria CA15 6AB
(090–081–2114)
*Helps those in trouble with the law
  through stress and depression –
  Midlands and Northern England.*

Centre For Professional Employment Counselling (CEPEC)
67 Jermyn St, London SW1Y 6NY
(01–930–0322)
*For managers with work-related
  problems who are sponsored by
  their employer. Also at Sundridge
  Park Management Centre, Brom-
  ley, Kent BR1 3JW
  (01–460–8585).*

Compassionate Friends
5 Lower Clifton Hill, Clifton,
  Bristol BS8 1BT
(0272–292778)
*Arranges friendly visits from people
  with similar problems.*

Gamblers Anonymous
17/23 Blantyre St, Cheyne Walk,
  London SW10
(01–352–3060)

Institute for Drug Dependence
3 Blackburn Rd, London NW6 1XA
(01–328–5541)

Institute of Psycho-sexual Medicine
11 Chandos St, Cavendish Square,
London WIM 9DE

Moneyline
(01–256–5312)
For advice about money worries.

National Association of Carers and
their Elderly Dependants
29 Chilworth Mews, London
W2 3RG
(01–262–1451/2)

National Marriage Guidance Coun-
cil
Little Church St, Rugby, Warwicks
CV21 3AP
(0788–73241)
*Will help couples and individuals
to obtain counselling.*

New Horizons
Choice Publications Ltd, 12 Bed-
ford Row, London WC1R 4DU
*For contact with local community
projects for retired people.*

Outsiders Club
PO Box 4ZB, London WIA 4ZB
(01–741–3332)
*For those who feel that some physi-
cal or social handicap makes it
difficult for them to make friends
and find someone to love.*

Parents Anonymous Helpline
9 Manor Gardens, Holloway Road,
London N7 6LA
(01–263–8918)

Relatives of the Mentally Ill
7 Selwyn Rd, Cambridge CB3 9EA

Redwood
83 Fordwych Rd, London NW2 3TL
(01–452–9261)
*National network of women's
sexuality and assertiveness
groups.*

Sexual and Personal Relationships
of the Disabled (SPOD)
286 Camden Rd, London N7 0BJ
(01–607–8851)

Stillbirth and Neonatal Death
Society (SANDS)
37 Christchurch Hill, London
NW3 1LA
(01–794–4601)

Women's Aid Federation
374 Gray's Inn Road, London WC1
(01–837–9316)
Phone 01–837–3762 for London in-
quiries only.
*For women suffering from vio-
lence.*

FURTHER READING

DEPRESSION

Depression by Dr Caroline Shreeve, Turnstone Press. Written from a medical perspective, very good on explaining how drugs can help or hinder. Practical advice.

Depression by Dr Paul Hauck, Sheldon Press. Friendly do-it-yourself advice from an experienced therapist.

I Can't Face Tomorrow by Dr Norman Keir, Thorsen's Publishing Group. Understanding suicide, and how to help people who feel suicidal.

Women and Depression by Deirdre Sanders, Sheldon Press. Practical self-help approach. Contains excellent address list.

Depression After Childbirth by Katharina Dalton, Oxford University Press. Post-natal depression.

Once a Month by Katharina Dalton, Fontana. Depression related to menstrual cycle.

How To Cope With Your Nerves by Dr Tony Lake, Sheldon Press. Explains mild and short-term depression and what to do about it.

ASSERTIVENESS

When I Say No I Feel Guilty by Manuel J. Smith, Bantam. The original bestseller on standing up to people.

A Woman In Your Own Right by Anne Dickson, Quartet. Assertiveness from a female perspective.

BEREAVEMENT, GRIEF AND DEPRESSION

Death and the Family by Lily Pincus, Faber Paperbacks. Classic work by noted psychotherapist concerning effects of grief on the family.

A Grief Observed by C. S. Lewis, Faber & Faber. Intensely moving account of personal experience of grief reported from a Christian perspective.

Living with Grief by Dr Tony Lake, Sheldon Press. Explains how people can reach a deeper commitment to life through their experience of loss.

The Courage To Grieve by Judy Tatelbaum, Heinemann.

Bereavement by Colin Murray Parkes, Pelican. Basically academic, but excellent and readable.

CHILD-CARE

Happy Children by Rudolf Dreikurs, Fontana. May seem a bit idealistic to
British readers, but still the best book for parents who want encouraged children.

COUNSELLING

Counselling Shop by Brigid Proctor. Comprehensive descriptions of many
of the kinds of counselling that are available.

SELF-UNDERSTANDING

Own Your Own Life by Richard G. Abell, Bantam. Very readable account
of how people can change.
The Integrity of the Personality by Anthony Storr, Pelican. For the more
intellectual reader.
Relationships by Dr Tony Lake, Michael Joseph.

TRANQUILLIZERS

How To Stop Taking Tranquillisers by Dr Peter Tyrer, Sheldon Press.
Women and Tranquillisers by Celia Haddon, Sheldon Press.